Enterprise Mobility Suite: Managing BYOD and Company-Owned Devices

Yuri Diogenes
Jeff Gilbert

PUBLISHED BY
Microsoft Press
A Division of Microsoft Corporation
One Microsoft Way
Redmond, Washington 98052-6399

Library of Congress Control Number: 2014955635
ISBN: 978-0-7356-9840-6

Printed and bound in the United States of America.

First Printing

Microsoft Press books are available through booksellers and distributors worldwide. If you need support related to this book, email Microsoft Press Book Support at mspinput@microsoft.com. Please tell us what you think of this book at http://www.microsoft.com/learning/booksurvey.

Acquisitions Editor: Karen Szall
Developmental Editor: Karen Szall
Editorial Production: Box Twelve Communications
Technical Reviewer: Randall Galloway; Technical Review services provided by Content Master, a member of CM Group, Ltd.
Copyeditor: Box Twelve Communications
Indexer Box Twelve Communications
Cover: Twist Creative • Seattle

Contents at a glance

Contents

What do you think of this book? We want to hear from you!

Microsoft is interested in hearing your feedback so we can continually improve our
books and learning resources for you. To participate in a brief online survey, please visit:

microsoft.com/learning/booksurvey

Chapter 7   Data access and protection   127

Chapter 8   Implementing data protection   149

What do you think of this book? We want to hear from you!

Microsoft is interested in hearing your feedback so we can continually improve our
books and learning resources for you. To participate in a brief online survey, please visit:

microsoft.com/learning/booksurvey

Foreword

Of all the books you'll read about the Enterprise Mobility Suite, this one is probably the first. In my opinion, it is also the most comprehensive to date.

Enterprise Mobility Management—the thing that EMS so brilliantly supports and empowers—is one of today's defining trends, and it is the core area of focus for some of the most brilliant software architects and developers in the tech industry. The reason is obvious: No other technological development will have a greater impact on the way we live and work than our current device ubiquity.

From an IT perspective, the number of devices your users want to use, the volume of data they access, and protecting those corporate assets (and the end users themselves) are just a handful of the incredibly serious issues you must face every day. This reality is what makes EMS so exciting; it represents the intersection of great software architects with the IT teams working on the front lines of organizations all over the world. With this cloud-based technology, and by leveraging things like Machine Learning from the cloud, the feedback loop is faster than ever. Now you can enable your users in ways you never have been able to in the past.

In this book you'll see—in practical terms and examples—how to make these devices and the people using them dramatically more productive, more connected, and more secure. From the back end of your infrastructure (Microsoft Intune, Azure Active Directory Premium, Azure AD RMS) to the apps your end users interact with every day (Office 365), EMS is an incredibly sophisticated set of tools that dramatically simplify many previously intractable technical challenges.

The Enterprise Mobility Suite is where I believe a cloud-first, mobile-first perspective really takes shape. The speed of business, the constant movement of workers and data, and the need to keep innovating are all delivered with the entirely service-based solutions offered by the EMS. It's powerful, reliable, and offers you the cross-platform functionality that's required to help you successfully and optimistically bridge your organization's past and future.

Jeff and Yuri have spent an exhaustive amount of time with every corner of the Enterprise Mobility Suite, and this book will prepare you to use it to solve the unique challenges your organization is facing today—and to plan ahead for your organization's long-term success.

Brad

Brad Anderson, Microsoft Corporate VP, Enterprise Client & Mobility,
@InTheCloudMSFT

Introduction

This book provides you with an introduction to the Enterprise Mobility Suite (EMS). In it, you are put in the driver's seat through scenario-based content covering each of the independent technologies that make up EMS: Microsoft Azure AD Premium, Azure Rights Management Services (RMS), and Microsoft Intune. Throughout the chapters, we guide you through the process of implementing EMS to support Mobile Device Management (MDM) of both company-owned devices and personally-owned devices in your enterprise environment.

The scenarios described in this book are truly end-to-end. Starting with enabling hybrid identity, you will quickly learn how to secure corporate data access, protect your employees' personal information, manage iOS, Android, and Windows devices, and, finally, how to monitor and perform basic troubleshooting of all EMS components.

The target audience for this book is comprised of enterprise IT Pros who are either charged with implementing EMS for their organizations or just want to learn more about the technologies that are included in EMS. While it is not possible to cover every aspect and nuance of the technologies included in EMS in a single book, we have attempted to include the content we believe will provide you with the solid foundation you will need as you begin your own EMS implementation journey.

Acknowledgments

The authors would like to thank Karen Szall and the entire Microsoft Press team for their support in this project, Brad Anderson for writing the foreword of this book, and all of our Microsoft colleagues who contributed by reviewing this book: Ben Hawken, Simon May, Robert Mazzoli, Sonia Wadhwa, Eddie Bowers, Keith Brintzenhofe, Marsha Shoemaker, Taylor Thomson, Ken Hoff, Gil Lapid Shafriri, Debbie Furtado, and Stacey Ellingson. We would also like to thank the Microsoft MVPs who reviewed this book: Kent Agerlund, Kenny Buntinx, Peter Daalmans, John Marcum, Torsten Meringer, Stefan Schörling, and Steve Thompson.

Yuri Diogenes   I would also like to thank my wife and daughters for their endless support and understanding; my great God for giving me strength and keep guiding my path; my friend and co-author Jeff Gilbert (without you this project would not have been possible—thanks); my great friends and former co-authors

Tom Shinder and Jim Harrison (you both keep inspiring me to write); my former managers Kathy Watanabe and Jason Whitmarsh for their support when I joined the team; and last, but not least, my parents for working hard to give me an education, which is the foundation that I use every day to keep moving forward in my career.

Jeff Gilbert   I would also like to thank my wife and kids for their support in always lending a sympathetic ear to my excited technical ramblings—which I'm sure sounded like a foreign language to them. This book could not have been possible without the help of Yuri Diogenes, my co-author and the one who inspired me to join him on this journey. I'd also like to thank all those whom I work with at Microsoft and my friends in the systems management IT community who have always supported me and given focus to the work I do every day.

Free ebooks from Microsoft Press

From technical overviews to in-depth information on special topics, the free ebooks from Microsoft Press cover a wide range of topics. These ebooks are available in PDF, EPUB, and Mobi for Kindle formats, ready for you to download at:

http://aka.ms/mspressfree

Check back often to see what is new!

Microsoft Virtual Academy

Build your knowledge of Microsoft technologies with free expert-led online training from Microsoft Virtual Academy (MVA). MVA offers a comprehensive library of videos, live events, and more to help you learn the latest technologies and prepare for certification exams. You'll find what you need here:

http://www.microsoftvirtualacademy.com

Errata, updates, & book support

We've made every effort to ensure the accuracy of this book and its companion content. You can access updates to this book—in the form of a list of submitted errata and their related corrections—at:

http://aka.ms/EMSdevice/errata

If you discover an error that is not already listed, please submit it to us at the same page.

If you need additional support, email Microsoft Press Book Support at *mspinput@microsoft.com*.

Please note that product support for Microsoft software and hardware is not offered through the previous addresses. For help with Microsoft software or hardware, go to *http://support.microsoft.com*.

We want to hear from you

At Microsoft Press, your satisfaction is our top priority, and your feedback our most valuable asset. Please tell us what you think of this book at:

http://aka.ms/tellpress

The survey is short, and we read every one of your comments and ideas. Thanks in advance for your input!

Stay in touch

Let's keep the conversation going! We're on Twitter: *http://twitter.com/MicrosoftPress*.

## Chapter 1

Enabling a mobile workforce

The catchy phrase "work from anywhere" has evolved throughout the years and nowadays working from anywhere is the standard for many industries. However, as consumers started to use their own gadgets more and more to perform work-related tasks, "working anywhere and from any device" has become the new vision for many enterprises in a mobile-first, cloud-first world. This chapter explains why it is important for companies to develop an effective strategy for embracing a mobile workforce and also explains how the paradigm shift caused by the Bring Your Own Device (BYOD) trend impacts the overall strategy to securely adopt a mobile workforce.

The shift towards mobility

When companies started to understand the value of cloud computing—particularly as it related to how they could leverage its resources to be more agile and to reduce costs—they also discovered that users were already consuming cloud resources on their own devices. Cloud-based apps are intended to run on all types of portable devices. Also, cloud-based apps are usually programmed to run on several major operating systems, a strategy that drives rapid adoption from consumers. In this new era of Enterprise IT—also referred to by Gartner[1] as the "Third Era of Enterprise IT"—enterprise users not only demand agility, they demand a substantial increase in productivity.

While you might think that this concept is new, the fact is that this mobility phenomenon has been growing for at least the past seven years. A 2008 IDC study sponsored by Microsoft and performed by International Data Corporation (IDC) called Mobility Solutions in Enterprise-Sized Businesses: Quantifying the Return on Investment[2] revealed that the Return of Investment (ROI) with the use of mobility technologies pays off. So the question becomes, "What strategy should be implemented to support a mobile workforce and remain competitive in the marketplace?"

A 2014 survey[3] published by IDG Enterprise Consumerization of IT in the Enterprise (CITE) suggests that the consumerization of IT maximizes the capabilities of mobility and

---

[1] For more information about the Third Era of Enterprise IT, visit *http://www.gartner.com/newsroom/id/2649419*.

[2] You can read the entire report at *http://aka.ms/MobileROI*.

[3] You can read the entire survey at *http://www.idgenterprise.com/report/idg-enterprise-consumerization-of-it-in-the-enterprise-study-2014*.

empowers users. This survey documents several key findings. The following two key findings specifically address the trends for IT and mobile workforces; these key findings are the core foundation of this book:

- The proliferation of user-owned devices requires companies to adjust their policies and invest in Mobile Device Management (MDM) capabilities in order to maintain control over the devices while ensuring users can remain productive.
- Security is a key element to consider throughout the lifecycle of mobile devices.

These findings reinforce the fact that while CEOs are willing to enable users to be more productive by using their own mobile devices, the IT department must remain in control of those devices to ensure the company's data is protected.

The challenges of enabling enterprise mobility

To address the challenges that comes with enabling mobility in your company, you must understand the four elements of an enterprise mobility strategy (see Figure 1-1):

- Users
- Devices
- Apps
- Data

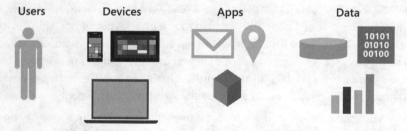

FIGURE 1-1 The four elements of an enterprise mobility strategy

When you embrace a mobile workforce, you not only must consider the user and the device he wants to use, you must consider how the apps that will be consumed will be affected by being on a mobile device. Even more importantly, you need to consider how to ensure that the company data remains secure. To effectively manage security of mobile devices, you should be sure to incorporate security into each of the four elements referenced in Figure 1-1. Focusing on each of the elements will help you to better address each challenge in a scenario-based approach. You want to ensure that your overall strategy is compliant with your business requirements while meeting the user's expectation about how she will perform at work using the device or devices of her choice.

Now that you know the elements, Figure 1-2 expands on the elements shown in Figure 1-1 and shows the three core scenarios that you will use throughout the entire book:

1. Enable users to choose their devices.

2. Unify the management of applications and devices

3. Protect corporate data.

By using this approach, you will be able to understand the challenges that must be addressed by your company before you embrace mobility.

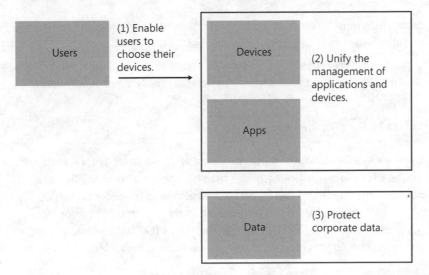

FIGURE 1-2 The three categories of challenges

As shown in Figure 1-2, the three core scenarios are bound to one or more of the elements shown in Figure 1-1. The following list explains the issues that must be addressed as part of your enterprise mobility strategy:

1. Enable users to choose their devices

   - Users want to use their own devices to access both their personal data and their work-related data/apps.

   - Users want access to these elements from anywhere.

   - While CEOs want to fulfill user requirements in order to enable users to be productive, they also want their IT department to be in control of how users access company data.

2. Unify the management of applications and devices

   - Users must have a common identity to access applications and company resources from any device and from anywhere.

   - IT must be able to manage, deploy, and maintain applications for all types of devices.

- IT must be able to manage company-owned devices as well as user-owned devices from a single location.

3. Protect corporate data

- Corporate data must be protected at all stages: while data is in the cloud, while data is at the company's datacenter, while data in the user's device, and while data is in transit between any (and all) of the aforementioned locations.

- Corporate data must be isolated and protected from a user's personal data while also securing a user's privacy.

- The IT department must be empowered to secure, classify, and protect the company's data while also maintaining regulatory compliance.

Throughout this book, these challenges will be used as examples for scenarios that explain how Enterprise Mobility Suite (EMS) can assist your company's efforts to enable a mobile workforce.

What about BYOD?

Your efforts to embrace a mobile workforce must include an effective strategy for handling the BYOD scenario. The BYOD scenario includes more than making your company "mobile ready;" it encompasses all the challenges and opportunities as well as the security risks of variations on the scenario. These variations will be explored in this chapter. Before you delve into the specific challenges involved with BYOD, think about why BYOD has become a "buzzword" and why companies should proceed cautiously when adopting BYOD.

Real World   The vendor-agnostic approach to BYOD

For the past two years, I've been delivering BYOD presentations that approach the topic from the architecture perspective and explain how to build a BYOD design with a vendor-agnostic approach. My first work on this field was released in April 2014 with the BYOD Design Considerations Guide (available at *http://aka.ms/BYODCG*), which features a collection of vendor-agnostic considerations regarding BYOD and how Microsoft technologies can help your company fulfill those requirements. The presentation that I delivered at TechEd North America 2014 was based on this paper; you can watch it at *http://aka.ms/byodtena14* and learn how to use a vendor-agnostic approach when developing your BYOD strategy.

To help IT professionals to think of BYOD as a problem domain that must have design considerations and choices aligned with company requirements, constraints, and vision, I also recorded a series of interviews (*http://ala.ms/byodseris*) for TechNet Radio. These materials can help you to plan, design and build your solution to address the BYOD challenges.

Yuri Diogenes
Senior Content Developer, CSI Enterprise Mobility Team, Microsoft Corporation

A November 2013 study by Gartner suggested that 20 percent of enterprise BYOD programs will fail before 2016. The study indicates programs will fail because of mobile device management measures that are too restrictive. This study shows that companies are moving towards the adoption of BYOD, but they are restricting access and thereby not necessarily realizing BYOD's full potential. Managing security is often a delicate balance. If your security policies aren't strict enough, you'll put corporate resources at risk. If your security policies are too strict, you might create an environment that becomes a tremendous challenge for the IT department to support, thereby adversely impacting your ROI. If your BYOD security produces a higher volume of help-desk calls from frustrated users, or, worse yet, if users are unable to perform their work, you might find that your organization needs to roll back to previous technology. As a result, BYOD becomes an enemy of the company. For this reason, you must ensure that your organization defines an effective BYOD strategy before BYOD is implemented or deployed.

In October 2014, a CheckPoint survey of 700 IT professionals showed mobile security incidents caused by BYOD had cost each organization more than $250,000 US to remediate[4]. These costs are likely to increase as more organizations adopt BYOD as part of their enterprise mobility strategy—underscoring the importance of understanding the challenges of adopting BYOD.

Understanding the challenges of BYOD

Before you can understand the challenges introduced by BYOD, you must first understand your own business requirements, constraints, regulatory compliance needs, and users' needs and goals. Unfortunately, this planning phase is often completely overlooked and gaps are found when the next phase—designing the solution—is underway. The best way to mitigate risk is to be aware of how your own company operates. The assumption here is that your company already has a security policy in place. What if that security strategy does not address the security challenges that BYOD introduces to the environment? The same rationale can be applied to your current management infrastructure. What if the existing management platform does not allow users to bring their own devices or does not provide access to company resources?

The industry that your company works in also plays an important role in how BYOD should be adopted. With BYOD, the device contains both the user's personal data and the company-owned data. This results in unique challenges for each industry. For instance, in a school environment, BYOD can be very helpful; to improving user productivity; however, the challenges can be very unique, as you will see in this section of the book.

> **MORE INFO**   Read "BYOD Devices - A Deployment Guide for Education" for a better understanding of the design considerations applicable to the education industry at *http://www.microsoft.com/en-us/download/details.aspx?id=39681.*

---

[4]   For more information about the core findings of this survey, visit *http://www.infosecurity-magazine.com/ news/byod-security-incident-costs/.*

There are privacy elements that must be considered for both the individual and the corporation. For this reason, it is very important to involve your legal department when planning the BYOD adoption. Employees must be aware that when they enroll in the BYOD program, the devices that they use might be subject to discovery in litigation. The personal devices they use at work could be examined not only by the employer but by the other party in a lawsuit. Of course, this will vary according to country/region and state laws. As shown in Figure 1-3, the Human Resources (HR), legal, and IT departments should be used as input when you're creating an Enterprise Mobility Strategy.

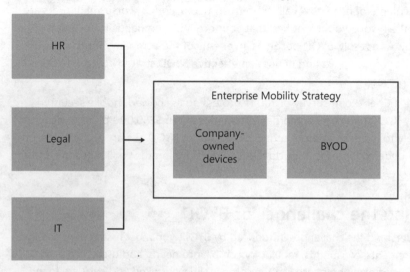

FIGURE 1-3 HR, Legal, and IT must review the enterprise mobility strategy

Awareness is an important aspect of BYOD. Employees need to be made aware of any legal risks involved in using their own devices for work-related tasks. For example, when employees travel internationally, their devices might be subject to search or seizure by border control agents. This affects not only the employee and his device but the company as well. Part of your self-assessment for BYOD adoption is making sure that the Legal and HR departments understand these scenarios. In this case, Legal should advise HR of the fact that an employee might forfeit certain rights to her personal device when using it for work. HR should also look for issues related to:

- Off-the-clock work for hourly employees and any potential compensation claims
- Local tax considerations
- Ownership of the telephone number (for a BYOD phone)

The responsibility for the loss of data on an employee-owned device can be proactively managed via policy. However, in a BYOD scenario it becomes more of a challenge. Deleting an employee's data from a personal device could have legal implications, so your organization should build a solid BYOD policy to protect itself. You should also be aware that some employees share their own devices with family members, and the shared use of employee-owned devices is one of the most pressing BYOD issues. This issue is very difficult to mitigate with policy. An employee sharing a BYOD device with his spouse invites the potential for serious issues, such as corporate data loss or security breaches.

Another BYOD scenario that must be addressed in partnership with HR and Legal is the situation whereby employees sell or recycle their own devices after those devices have been used to access company data. A common policy and technology strategy is to enable remote wiping of the device's data and require it as a condition of program participation.

IMPORTANT For policies to be effective, they must be well written, clearly communicated to employees, and enforced. Employees who are enrolling in a BYOD program must sign an agreement that holds them accountable for their actions.

The synergy among the HR, Legal and IT departments will help the company to better embrace enterprise mobility and address the challenges introduced by the BYOD scenario. In summary, the role of each department in this process is as follows:

- HR is responsible for developing policies for BYOD usage, selecting the people involved in setting those policies, as well as driving the training and compliance related to policies.
- Legal is responsible for identifying the information that can be accessed by specific individuals or groups and has input into policy development.
- IT implements the policies as directed by the HR and Legal departments, choosing the tools and technologies used to deliver the services, access resources, and protect data.

Understanding the Microsoft Device Strategy Framework

Figure 1-3 introduces the concept of two types of devices: company-owned device and user-owned device. However, there are variations in both ownership and management of the devices that make it necessary to expand the BYOD scenario to include the four core scenarios shown in Figure 1-4. These scenarios comprise the Microsoft Device Strategy Framework.

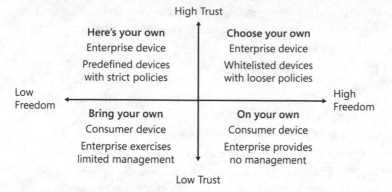

FIGURE 1-4 The Microsoft Device Strategy Framework

The scenarios shown in Figure 1-4 can be summarized as follows:

- **On your own**   In this model, employees provide their own devices. There are no security policies in place, no organizational management of the device, and any device is acceptable. This is a very open approach, but it presents the highest security risk.

- **Bring your own device**   This model includes two distinct variations on policy management:

  - Bring your own *unmanaged* device   In this model, employees provide their own devices, but as part of the company policy, the company does not manage those devices. The employees are responsible for implementing and managing company policies on their devices. This is a flexible policy but it presents security risks; some businesses might not have the resources to manage these risks.

  - Bring your own *managed* device   This is the most traditional format for BYOD. In this model, employees provide their own devices and the company enforces its policy to allow the devices to access company data. The device is fully managed by the company.

- **Choose your own device** (also called CYOD)   In this model, the company provides a mobile device to employees so those employees can perform their jobs remotely. The company often allows employees to choose from a list of approved devices that are fully compatible with the company's apps and management infrastructure.

- **Here's your own device**   In this model, the company has one device approved for the company's mobile platform and this device is provided to employees.

The landscape for enterprise mobility extends well beyond BYOD; you cannot assume enterprise mobility means BYOD only. There are many more elements that must be covered to completely embrace mobility and enable a mobile workforce. Each scenario has advantages and disadvantages that vary according to company requirements and goals.

MORE INFO For more information about the Microsoft Device Strategy Framework, see the blog post by the Enterprise Mobility Team at *http://blogs.technet.com/b/enterprise-mobility/archive/2014/10/08/looking-back-and-moving-forward-with-enterprise-mobility-suite-beyond-the-byod-scenario.aspx*.

Designing a strategy to enable a mobile workforce

This chapter has covered the factors that are driving enterprise mobility adoption and the core challenges you need to address when developing an enterprise mobility strategy. This section takes the elements shown in Figure 1-1 and explains how to use them to design an effective strategy to enable enterprise mobility.

Users

The first element is the user or employee. The user becomes a key element when companies start to move from a device-centric view to a user-centric view. Each user within your company has specific business needs; some have common business needs and some have unique business requirements. This part of the designing process is necessary to understand the user's profile. This is accomplished by defining *personas*. The following list provides examples of typical user profiles:

- **Executive** This persona expects the company to buy them whatever device they want to use as their primary device. An Executive isn't likely to be a BYOD user.

- **Mobile worker** This persona encompasses a large group of employees that are accustomed to using multiple devices.

- **Technical/field worker** This persona requires a robust device to perform their work. Usually, this type of user primarily accesses line of business (LOB) applications and email, and enters data into customer relationship management (CRM) tools.

- **Deskbound information worker** This persona uses a variety of devices and enrolls in the BYOD program. From taking notes in meetings on their own companion devices to potentially wanting to use their own machines while in the workplace, these users are likely to drive most of the BYOD adoptions in the company.

- **Remote information worker** This persona looks to optimize their workspace, blending personal priorities with company priorities. These users might be good candidates for the BYOD program.

Keep in mind that these are just some examples of user profiles for an enterprise. Different industries and business have different roles and requirements. It is important to identify the persona and comprehend the users' needs based on their roles. You will identify these roles as part of the company self-assessment, which should be done before you start designing the enterprise mobility strategy.

You also need to consider the persona distribution, which is based on two elements: autonomy and mobility. Figure 1-5 shows the rationale behind the persona distribution.

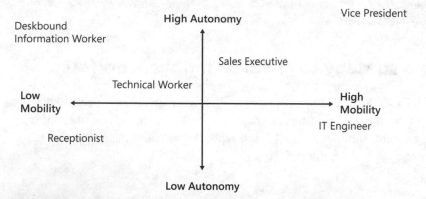

FIGURE 1-5 A persona distribution quadrant

This persona distribution relates to the user's work style and how the company can ensure that this user has what she needs to be productive. For example, some employees might always work at the same physical location (categorized as low mobility) while others might work at different branches, work from home, work from hotels, and so on (categorized as high mobility). The degree of autonomy is directly related to the balance between the freedom that the user needs to perform their business operations and the amount of restrictions added by the security policies.

Devices

Consider the type of devices that the company will allow. Access should be available from a broad set of device types, including managed devices, unmanaged devices, and consumer devices. Also, you should plan to include both Windows-based and non–Windows-based devices. Assuming your company will include a BYOD scenario, it is important to perform a survey of your employees to understand which devices they use and which operating systems they have installed on those devices.

When determining which devices will be supported by the company, carefully balance information security classification with the trustworthiness of the device and the point of connection. It is important to understand the device's capabilities and define how those devices will access corporate information. The required capabilities of each device might vary according to the company's security policy and business requirements. Figure 1-6 shows an example of some considerations regarding the device type and required capabilities. After you have defined the devices that will be supported, you need to define the required capabilities, such as data encryption, customization via policy, Mobile Device Management (MDM), and containerization.

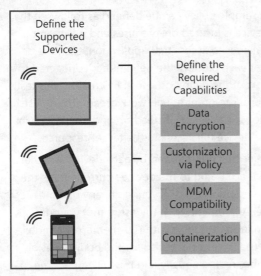

FIGURE 1-6 An example of device type selection based on required capabilities

It's important for the IT department to understand if the devices that will be supported by the company have these capabilities. Once the device type is established, you need to define the access level that the device will have based on pre-established variables. User, device, location, and data can be used as variables to define the user's experience when accessing corporate data. One variable, for example, can be the device's location. Your company policy might allow full network access only for devices that are located on-premises. When the device is located on-premises, it will have one set of policies applied to it; if it is coming from the cloud, it will have a more restrictive policy. *It is important to balance security with usability.* You don't want to enforce so much restriction that there is a negative effect on the user's productivity. If you find the right balance, you will increase productivity. Figure 1-7 shows an example of some of these variables.

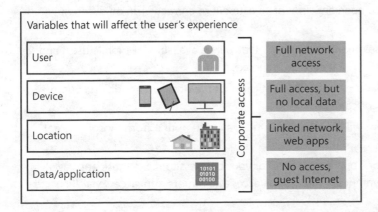

FIGURE 1-7 Examples of variables that will affect the user's experience while accessing corporate data

Using the diagram in Figure 1-7 as model, a sample policy can be defined as follows: if the device type is a Windows 8.1 phone and the device is located on-premises and it is trying to access an LOB application and the user has privileges to access that application, then the device should have full network access. Notice that each piece of the definition is connected to the next piece with "and," which makes each part of the definition a test. By creating this test, all answers to these questions must be true in order to grant full network access. These tests can vary. For example, your company might choose to use "or" instead of "and," which means only one requirement must be true to allow the device full access to the target resource.

Now that you have defined the key capabilities that are required by each device and the variables that will influence the user's experience according to the device's current state, the next important point to cover for the device is the supportability. If your company operates as a service provider, you could use a Service Level Agreement (SLA) to ensure that your users are aware of what to expect when they open an incident report with IT. An enterprise mobility strategy must include a plan to support the user's device and also set the boundaries of this support. The fact is that not all devices will be treated equally and this will impact the supportability boundaries. This should be very clear not only to the IT team but to the user as well. By knowing what to expect from support, you mitigate the possibility of user frustration when that user opens an incident report and her device has limited support.

Apps

Although the industry tends to put more emphasis on devices, apps are the main gateway to information access. If your company doesn't have mobile apps, embracing a mobile workforce won't be very productive. As part of your design considerations, you must understand the current LOB applications that are used by your employees, how these apps will behave on the different operating systems that you are about to support, as well as the user's skill level on each device that is approved by IT. When developing a strategy for apps, you must:

- Define which apps will be available for the users to consume using their devices
- Validate if those apps need any type of adjustment to correctly run on different platforms
- Perform a threat assessment on each app that will be available for mobile users and verify if there is any flaw that can lead to a security risk
- Mitigate potential flaws by fixing the root cause of the problem or adding counter-measures that can reduce the risk
- Verify how these apps will be available for user's consumption from those different devices
- Enumerate the options that are feasible for your business to make those apps available (for example, deployment via web portal, access via remote app, access via VPN, and so on)

During this exercise, you will identify different gaps and each gap should be documented in detail. The output of this design consideration for apps might induce you to upgrade your server infrastructure to support this new model or adopt cloud-based apps for your mobile users.

Data

Remember, the CEO wants to enable users to be productive from anywhere, using the device of their choice, while keeping company data secure. The key to a successful enterprise mobility adoption is to allow users to consume company resources without compromising the data. The considerations regarding data protection should include:

- A security envelope to protect the data
- Safety net policies that control access and reporting
- An additional level of authentication, such as multifactor authentication
- Business-driven policies for data protection
- A classification of data according to sensitivity and business impact
- Access control to data based on identity and role
- Data encryption

You should understand how data can be protected on different platforms. Also, you should understand each platform's capabilities so those capabilities can be leveraged to protect data. Some mobile platforms will use the principle of least privilege to protect and isolate data, such as the Windows Phone security model and its use of AppContainer as a secured isolation boundary.

> **MORE INFO**   To better understand the Windows Phone 8.1 security model, read the white paper at *http://www.microsoft.com/en-us/download/details.aspx?id=42509*.

While IT has full control over the data stored at the company's data center, the same level of assurance can be a challenge with unmanaged BYOD devices. How data will be stored in users' devices can directly impact how you choose to address data access and protection for enterprise mobility. Data encryption must be considered, and devices must allow IT to control when data encryption is enabled and for which types of data. Companies must review their policies and regulations to understand which types of data are allowed to leave the data-center and be at rest in remote devices' storage.

Protecting the data is not enough; you must monitor how this data has been accessed so you can take measures to mitigate potential breaches. Part of you enterprise mobility strategy includes data governance. Choosing the right management platform to monitor your data access and take actions based on what you are able to find via reporting capabilities should be a very important decision point to your company. With the assumption that users can access data from anywhere, you must be vigilant to potential patterns that can help your company understand that an attack is in place.

Threat mitigation

After evaluating each element of your enterprise mobility strategy, you can now perform a threat modelling exercise to understand the interactions between each component and identify threats that might occur during those interactions that require mitigation. Using the core elements of Figure 1-1, you can determine who should be allowed to access the data. The first goal during threat mitigation is to reduce the attack surface by disallowing direct access to some of those elements. Figure 1-8 shows an example of the core elements of an enterprise mobility strategy. In the Before scenario, each element has direct access to the data. In the After scenario, direct access is limited to Apps only.

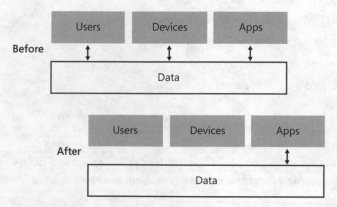

FIGURE 1-8 Reducing the attack surface by limiting direct access to the data

Another step of the threat mitigation process is to understand the risks on each interaction between these components. In Figure 1-8, for example, what risks are present when these apps have direct access to the data? You might conclude that the following actions must be performed:

- For apps to have access to data, the communication channel must be encrypted
- All mobile apps should be developed using a security development lifecycle
- Data at rest on the application server must be encrypted

To assist you through the process of understanding the risks of each interaction, you can leverage the Microsoft Threat Modeling Tool. Although this tool was created for another purpose, the rationale behind threat modeling is the same for interactions between the components of this model. Once you build the diagram and the data flows through the components, you can generate a report that will highlight the potential threats that must be mitigated. Figure 1-9 shows an example of this report.

MORE INFO You can download the Microsoft Threat Modeling Tool at *http://www.micro-soft.com/en-us/download/details.aspx?id=42518.*

Interaction: IPsec

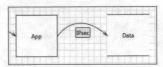

1. Spoofing of Destination Data Store Data   [State: Not Started] [Priority: High]

Category: Spoofing is when a process or entity is something other than its claimed identity. Examples include substituting a process, a file, website or a network address.

Description: Data may be spoofed by an attacker and this may lead to data being written to the attacker's target instead of Data. Consider using a standard authentication mechanism to identify the destination data store.

Justification: <no mitigation provided>

2. Lower Trusted Subject Updates Logs   [State: Not Started] [Priority: High]

Category: Repudiation threats involve an adversary denying that something happened.

Description: If you have trust levels, is anyone other outside of the highest trust level allowed to log? Letting everyone write to your logs can lead to repudiation problems. Only allow trusted code to log.

Justification: <no mitigation provided>

3. Data Logs from an Unknown Source   [State: Not Started] [Priority: High]

Category: Repudiation threats involve an adversary denying that something happened.

Description: Do you accept logs from unknown or weakly authenticated users or systems? Identify and authenticate the source of the logs before accepting them.

Justification: <no mitigation provided>

FIGURE 1-9 A report generated using the Microsoft Threat Modeling Tool

This report also categorizes the threats according to priorities, which can also help you understand which threats should be addressed first. When you finish this designing process for enterprise mobility, you should have:

- A full understanding of how your company will benefit from the adoption of enterprise mobility
- A vendor-agnostic design of your enterprise mobility solution
- A threat mitigation report with core points that must be addressed during the implementation
- A list of requirements that must be met by the vendor

Chapter 2

Introducing the Enterprise Mobility Suite

I n the previous chapter, you had the opportunity to learn about enterprise mobility and how to embrace a mobile workforce. Microsoft offers a suite of cloud services called Enterprise Mobility Suite (EMS) to address the enterprise mobility challenges. The plan is to help organizations enable their users to be productive on the devices they love while protecting company data. This chapter describes EMS and each of its three cloud services, as well as the considerations for implementing each service.

Understanding the EMS solution

Chapter 1 introduced the four elements (users, devices, apps, and data) involved in the enterprise mobility strategy. These elements will be used as examples throughout the book. Knowing that the core of your enterprise mobility solution must include these four elements will make it easier for you to understand how EMS can enable organizations to embrace a mobile workforce. EMS has three "pillars" that support the EMS elements (see Figure 2-1):

- Hybrid identity
- Mobile Device Management (MDM)
- Data protection

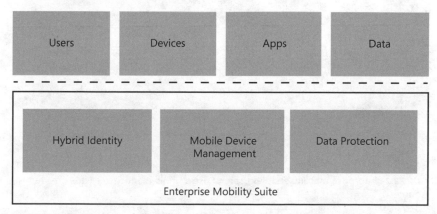

FIGURE 2-1 Enterprise mobility pillars are the foundation of EMS

These pillars are essential pieces of the enterprise mobility solution. For each pillar, EMS a cloud service that provides the capabilities that are required to achieve the demands established by each pillar. These pillars and the related cloud service for each are shown in Table 2-1.

TABLE 2-1 The cloud services for each EMS pillar

Pillar	Service
Hybrid identity management	Microsoft Azure Active Directory Premium
Mobile Device Management	Microsoft Intune
Data Protection	Microsoft Azure Rights Management Service

Establishing a hybrid identity

It is fundamentally important to mobile users that they have access to what they need to perform their work, regardless of where they might be located. However, it is also fundamentally important for the IT department to understand who is trying to access the information and to validate the level of authorization necessary to access the information. This is where identity becomes one of the most important aspects in an enterprise mobility solution.

In addition, it is important to allow users to consume cloud-based Software as a Service (SaaS) apps approved by the company without requiring users to memorize multiple credentials. As you know, increasing the number of credentials (usernames and passwords) leads to problems for the users. They might forget one credential or they might start using weak passwords to access other apps, which can lead to a security breach. Figure 2-2 shows how a common identity can be important to maintaining a seamless experience across on-premises and cloud resources.

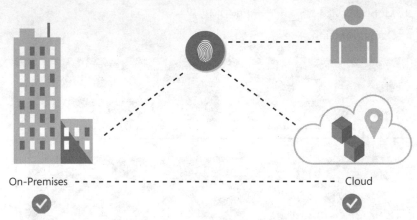

On-Premises --- Cloud

FIGURE 2-2 Enterprise mobility enables users to use a single identity to access on-premises and cloud resources

Not every company has a robust infrastructure to keep remote access on-premises. Most of the time, the budget needs to include funding for more than just the maintenance of remote access or of a VPN appliance; your budget also has to include an IT team prepared to maintain this infrastructure. In this scenario, cloud computing can be a vital asset for the company. Even if the organization doesn't plan to fully migrate to a cloud environment, it can realize the benefits of adopting a hybrid solution. An IT administrator responsible for maintaining a hybrid environment should be able to manage resources located on-premises and in the cloud while preserving a seamless user-authentication experience. For this reason, EMS uses the Hybrid Identity model, which enables organizations to leverage their current investments in identity management located on-premises to authenticate and authorize access to users while those users have the capability to integrate with a cloud-based identity directory.

While these are foundational aspects of an identity solution for an enterprise mobility strategy, the following items are other key requirements that must be fulfilled in any identity solution:

- Organizations need to enable users to use a single set of identity on their devices of choice to access resources in the cloud and on-premises.

- Organizations that are not going to fully migrate to the cloud require a hybrid environment in order to leverage cloud-computing capabilities while keeping their sensitive data on-premises.

- Organizations need to enhance their security by implementing multi-factor authentication (MFA) for users accessing resources from the cloud.

- Organizations need to be able to manage their user's identity-to-identity suspicious activities.

The EMS service responsible for addressing these requirements is called Microsoft Azure Active Directory Premium. Chapter 3 covers the Azure AD Premium capabilities and Chapter 4 covers how to implement some of these capabilities.

It is important to identify which options meet the requirements for your organization to implement hybrid identity. When deciding which option your organization should use, ensure that the option that you choose can evolve as new requirements arise. Even if your organization does not have a hybrid IT environment, the solution that will be implemented should be flexible enough to meet the requirements when it is necessary to integrate the business with cloud services.

> **MORE INFO**   For a list of advantages and disadvantages to using each identity option, read section 4.3.3 of the BYOD Design Considerations Guide at *http://aka.ms/byodcg*.

Managing mobile devices

Another EMS pillar is Mobile Device Management. This pillar has direct correlation to how your organization will administer mobile devices, deploy apps, and help secure organizational data. Organizations that are planning to embrace mobility need to enable IT to view and manage PCs, mobile devices, servers, and virtual machines that are both corporate-connected and cloud-based connected. It is also imperative that the management platform is capable of performing inventory, applying policies, and distributing software to a wide range of devices across multiple platforms. Figure 2-3 illustrates the challenge for IT admins, where they need to be able to manage all these devices from a single location.

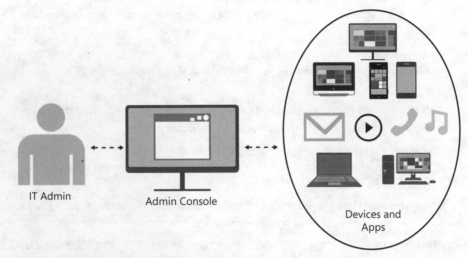

FIGURE 2-3 IT admins need to manage multiple devices and apps across multiple platforms from a single location

Device management requirements

As discussed in Chapter 1, BYOD is one vital scenario in the enterprise mobility space. To securely embrace this solution, management must enable IT to define and deploy configuration policies specific to each mobile device platform that will help meet compliance requirements and at the same time protect employee privacy and data. Mobile users will use a variety of devices to consume data and apps that are controlled by the organization. The management platform must enable IT to publish or deploy applications to users' corporate or personal devices based on pre-defined policies. Ideally the management platform should be as unobtrusive to the user as possible. The IT administrator needs to empower users to be productive without impeding their ability to perform their work. IT administrators must be able to perform the following device management tasks:

- Manage updates
- Monitor and trigger alerts proactively

- Perform hardware and software inventory
- Set security policies
- Distribute software
- Provide remote assistance
- Help protect PCs from malware
- Remotely wipe and selectively wipe mobile devices

As you can see, device management is an important part of your enterprise mobility strategy and there are many requirements that must be fulfilled. Within EMS, Microsoft Intune is responsible for addressing these requirements. Chapter 5 covers the Microsoft Intune capabilities and Chapter 6 covers how to implement some of these capabilities.

Device management considerations

You need to ensure that the device management option you select meets the requirements for your organization *before* you implement the device management solution. By default, Microsoft Intune is the option available with EMS. However, you must evaluate the following approaches to device management and define your approach before you implement it:

- Unify the on-premises device management solution with the cloud-based management solution
- Manage the mobile devices separately from the on-premises devices using the cloud-based device management solution

If your organization decides to unify the management environment, you must evaluate this integration prior to implementing it. A different set of designing and planning options must be reviewed before you can properly deploy this solution according to the organization's business requirements.

> **MORE INFO**   For a list of advantages and disadvantage to using each device management option, read section 4.4 of the BYOD Design Considerations Guide at *http://aka.ms/byodcg*.

Protecting data

As part of creating your enterprise mobility strategy, policies and data classifications must be defined as part of the overall data protection solution. Once IT validates the users' identities, the next step is to apply additional conditions to the types of devices that are able to access the information and apps provided by the organization. Organizations that are planning to embrace mobility need to ensure that their data is protected no matter where the data is located (on-premises, in the cloud, or on the user's device). Ideally, corporate files should be protected even when you copy them to another folder or device or when you share the folder in which the files are located. Figure 2-4 illustrates the many areas where data must be protected.

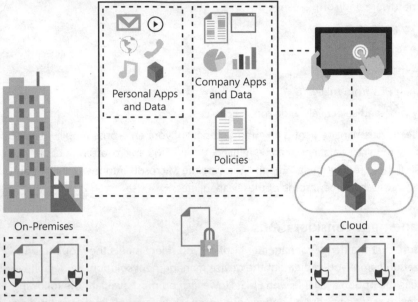

FIGURE 2-4 IT admins needs to protect data in all locations

As shown in Figure 2-4, data protection must be applied on-premises, in transit (usually done by using encryption), in the cloud, and at the user's device. The important aspect of data protection at the user's device is the isolation of personal data from the organization's data. IT admins must be able to, at any moment, remove the organization's apps and data from the user's device without harming the user's personal files and apps.

Mitigating risk

Many organizations are concerned about embracing mobility because their perception is that the likelihood that data leakage will occur will increase. While this is a fair assumption, the enterprise mobility strategy must mitigate this potential risk by ensuring that the data protection solution is able to:

- Protect all file types
- Protect files sent via email
- Protect data located in all commonly used devices, not just Windows computers
- Support data protection for on-premises services as well as in the cloud (SaaS such as Office 365)
- Scale across your organization as needed
- Adhere to regulatory requirements
- Allow IT to keep control of the data
- Maintain the users' abilities to interact and protect their own documents

EMS addresses these requirements through the Azure Rights Management Services (RMS). Chapter 7 covers Azure RMS capabilities and Chapter 8 covers how to implement some of these capabilities.

Data protection considerations

While Azure RMS specifically addresses data protection, there are other capabilities distributed among the other pillars (hybrid identity and device management) that are all part of the data protection solution. Remember, data is the core of your solution; therefore you should apply the defense-in-depth approach to add multiple layers of security to ensure total protection of the data. Defense-in-depth should leverage not only the data protection capabilities offered by EMS but also the built-in capabilities available from each platform, such as the Windows operating system.

Table 2-2 shows the different layers of security that are involved before the user accesses the data. Security considerations for each layer are part of the defense-in-depth strategy to protect the data itself.

TABLE 2-2 Defense-in-depth approach for data protection

Security layer	Includes...
Data	Access control list (ACL), encryption (Encrypting File System [EFS], BitLocker), data classification with RMS
Application	Application design using the security development lifecycle, antivirus, application hardening
Host	Operating system hardening, authentication, update management, host intrusion detection system
Internal network	Network segmentation, network encryption (Internet Protocol security [IPSec]), network intrusion detection system
Perimeter	Firewalls, network access control, network access protection (NAP)
Physical security	Guards, locks, tracking devices, surveillance cameras
People, policies, processes	Security awareness training, documentation, banners, warning signs

EMS activation process

While EMS is a solution for enterprise mobility adoption, this solution is the aggregation of separate cloud services (Azure AD Premium, Microsoft Intune, and Azure Rights Management). Therefore, there is no procedure to install EMS; what you will do is a single activation process. Once action is completed, the additional steps to configure each part of the solution are unique to each cloud service. The EMS activation process can be summarized in three steps:

1. Sign up for EMS.
2. Activate the license plan.
3. Activate access.

MORE INFO   For more details about each step, you can download the EMS Activation Guide at *http://aka.ms/emsaguide*.

Real World   A glimpse of EMS licensing

EMS is a per-user subscription that includes user subscriptions for Intune, Azure AD Premium, and Azure Rights Management. An Intune subscription provides rights to manage five devices per user subscription. At the time of this book's publication, EMS is available for purchase as part of the Microsoft Enterprise Cloud Suite via a Microsoft Enterprise Agreement. As part of an Enterprise Agreement, organizations can acquire EMS as an add-on subscription when adding to existing CoreCAL or ECAL licenses with software assurance (SA) or they can purchase EMS as a full subscription for users not covered by SA. The three services are also available as individual subscriptions via direct web purchase and through the Microsoft Volume licensing programs: Microsoft Products and Services Agreement (MPSA) and Open.

Stacey Ellingson
Director, Business Planning, Microsoft Corporation

MORE INFO   To see the latest information about EMS Licensing options, go to *http://www.microsoft.com/en-us/server-cloud/products/enterprise-mobility-suite/buy.aspx*

Embracing a mobile workforce scenario

To help you understand how each EMS service will be used as part of the enterprise mobility solution, the following scenario will be used throughout this book. Each implementation chapter will reference this scenario and will implement one or more of the requirements that are described in this section. At the end of this book you will have the completed solution implemented and all requirements for the fictitious organization shown in Figure 2-5 will be fulfilled.

FIGURE 2-5 The logo of the fictitious organization that will be used in this book

Blue Yonder Airlines has made a recent acquisition and is in the process of expanding its business throughout different regions of the country. As result of the acquisition, many of the new employees will be working remotely from multiple time zones and they will be changing geographic locations. With so many employees traveling throughout the world, it is becoming an overwhelming challenge for the centralized IT staff to manage access to organizational resources.

In addition, many of the new Blue Yonder Airlines employees are complaining that it takes too long to obtain the security access to apps that they need to use in order to be productive or that they simply cannot access the app on their devices. When IT investigated these issues, they discovered that more and more Blue Yonder Airlines employees are accessing their corporate email, company applications, and company data from many different types of personal devices (rather than from company-owned computers). Recently, one employee's unmanaged personal device became compromised with malware and this malware infected a file located at the corporate office, causing a potential data breach. Fortunately, IT was able to contain the issue and clean the file system before any harm was done. However, it alerted the organization to the fact that it needs to resolve its resource access and device management problems as soon as possible in order to keep its employees productive and organization's data secure.

After researching BYOD trends and user productivity studies, the leadership team at Blue Yonder Airlines concluded that it needs to embrace BYOD and implement an enterprise mobility management solution as soon as possible. The team knows it must first draft a BYOD policy and ensure employees are aware of the policy before employees use their personal devices to access company data. However, in addition to creating the BYOD policy, the leadership team must also meet several business requirements.

Currently, Blue Yonder Airlines has the following infrastructure on-premises:

- Active Directory is running on-premises with hundreds of users authenticating on a daily basis
- Exchange Server 2013 is running with users accessing their mailboxes via Outlook client, mobile devices (ActiveSync) and Outlook Web App (OWA)
- There is no Systems Management technology implemented on-premises
- The current security policies do not cover BYOD scenarios

Blue Yonder Airlines' goals with this project are to enable enterprise mobility to ensure that its employees are more productive and that they can work from anywhere using the devices of their choice while also protecting company data and resources. Blue Yonder Airlines established the following requirements in order to consider this project successful:

- Leverage its on-premises investment in Windows Server Active Directory and Azure to deliver a hybrid identity that enables users to be productive while leaving IT in control
- Implement SSO so that users need only one name and one password to access both on-premises and cloud-based software and services

- Enable a seamless user experience for users transitioning from on-premises to the cloud by providing a consistent look and feel across all managed websites and services.

- Require users to register information that is required to enable MFA before getting access to company resources

- Require users to register devices before accessing company resources

- Enable users to access and use centrally managed SaaS apps from a secure location

- Enable user self-service to reduce help-desk calls and empower users to manage their profiles, passwords, and delegated Azure AD group memberships

- Enable IT to easily monitor and protect access to organizational resources

- Manage MFA for mobile users who are accessing company resources

- Ensure that all major platforms (Windows, Android, and iOS) are managed and supported by the company

- Ensure that policy enforcement is available for company-owned devices as well as user-owned devices (BYOD)

- Ensure that data is protected and classified

- Establish ways to mitigate issues related to data leakage on mobile devices

- Minimize investment in implementing an on-premises infrastructure

- Implement EMS with as little administrative overhead as possible while still enabling centralized reporting to monitor organizational activity and services.

## Chapter 3

Hybrid identity

Windows Server Active Directory and Forefront Identity Manager (FIM) have long been the standard for on-premises identity management, but in a mobile-first, cloud-first world, the concept of user identity must be expanded to include identity for cloud-based applications and management spanning multiple services. The Microsoft hybrid identity solution spans on-premises and cloud-based capabilities to create a single user identity for authentication and authorization regardless of where the user is. By easily extending your local directories into Microsoft Azure Active Directory (Azure AD) through directory synchronization, hybrid identity provides users with one username and password to remember and enables authentication and self-service scenarios to keep users happy and productive while also protecting company information.

Everything starts with identity and it will be one of the foundations of your enterprise mobility strategy. Whether you are logging into your mobile device or your Software as a Service (SaaS) app, your identity is the key to gaining access to everything. This chapter discusses how Azure AD works with your on-premises Active Directory to provide a comprehensive identity and access management hybrid identity solution as part of the Enterprise Mobility Suite. In this chapter, you will learn about the various aspects and capabilities of Azure AD Premium that support hybrid identity and the tools used to synchronize on-premises directories with the cloud in preparation for the implementation guidance you will learn in Chapter 4.

Cloud identity with Azure AD Premium

Chances are that you are already familiar with Windows Server Active Directory and how it is used to provide identity management. That being the case, you might think that Azure AD is the cloud-version of the on-premises solution that has become the bedrock for so many enterprises, but Azure AD is really much more than a domain controller in the sky. In addition to providing identity management, Azure AD is also a complete access management cloud solution. Azure AD handles identity governance, manages access to applications, and also provides a standards-based platform for developers to build their own applications without having to worry about how identity will be factored in because Azure AD will handle that for them. Enterprise businesses today require a solution that can verify a user's identity across multiple devices to give them access to apps and resources in a consistent manner. That solution is cloud identity with Azure AD Premium.

Azure AD Premium is included with the Enterprise Mobility Suite and, in addition to the rich features supported by Azure Active Directory Free and Azure Active Directory Basic editions,[1] it enables bonus advanced features to your directory that help empower enterprises with more demanding identity and access management requirements. When you use Azure AD Premium, you can perform write-back of object attributes from Azure AD to your on-premises directories as well as do things like view advanced security reports and alerts, enable multi-factor authentication, and provide self-service group and password reset management.

Azure AD Premium advanced security reports and alerts

Azure AD Premium access and usage reports[2] are based on machine learning and allow you to easily monitor and protect access to your Azure AD tenant resources. Using these reports, you can view information that will help to secure your organization's Azure AD directory. The data collected and displayed by Azure AD Premium Reports can be used to better determine where possible security risks might be present so that they can be addressed and mitigated. In addition, there are other reports that provide analytics on device access and application usage so that you can better manage resources.

To view the reports available for you to run, simply go to the Reports tab of your Azure AD directory as shown in Figure 3-1. To run a report, just click the report name in the list and you will see a detailed page for that specific report. In addition to viewing the report, you can also download a copy of it as a compressed, Comma Separated Values (CSV) format for offline viewing or backup purposes.

> **TIP** If you see a section called Premium Reports at the bottom of the Reports tab for your directory containing reports, the account you are logged in as has not been granted an Azure AD Premium license.

The remainder of this section describes the premium reports that are currently available for you to use in managing your Azure AD objects and resources in addition to those available by default.

---

[1] You can learn more about the different versions of Azure AD at *http://azure.microsoft.com/en-us/pricing/details/active-directory/*.

[2] You can learn more about Azure AD Premium access and usage reports at *http://msdn.microsoft.com/en-us/library/azure/dn283934.aspx*.

REPORT	DESCRIPTION
⊿ ANOMALOUS ACTIVITY	
Sign ins from unknown sources	May indicate an attempt to sign in without being traced.
Sign ins after multiple failures	May indicate a successful brute force attack.
Sign ins from multiple geographies	May indicate that multiple users are signing in with the same account.
Sign ins from IP addresses with suspicious activity	May indicate a successful sign in after a sustained intrusion attempt.
Sign ins from possibly infected devices	May indicate an attempt to sign in from possibly infected devices.
Irregular sign in activity	May indicate events anomalous to users' sign in patterns.
Users with anomalous sign in activity	Indicates users whose accounts may have been compromised.
⊿ ACTIVITY LOGS	
Audit report	Audited events in your directory
Password reset activity	Provides a detailed view of password resets that occur in your organization.
Password reset registration activity	Provides a detailed view of password reset registrations that occur in your organization.
Groups activity	Provides an activity log to all group related activity in your directory
⊿ INTEGRATED APPLICATIONS	
Application usage	Provides a usage summary for all SaaS applications integrated with your directory.
Account provisioning activity	Provides a history of attempts to provision accounts to external applications.
Account provisioning errors	Indicates an impact to users' access to external applications.

FIGURE 3-1 Azure AD Premium reports available in the Azure portal

Anomalous activity reports

Azure AD Premium anomaly reports alert you to suspicious sign-in behaviors and include the following reports:

- **Sign ins from IP addresses with suspicious activity**   This report can be used to find a successful sign-in after a sustained intrusion attempt.

- **Sign ins from possibly infected devices**   This report indicates an attempt to sign in from possibly infected devices.

- **Irregular sign in activity**   This report shows events that might indicate anomalous patterns in user signs.

- **Users with anomalous sign in activity**   This report shows information about user accounts that might have been compromised.

> **TIP**   You can scope the interval to the last twenty-four hours, seven days, or thirty days for all of the above Azure AD Premium Reports.

Activity logs

These Azure AD Premium reports provide activity logs about audited events that can be scoped to a specific number of days and include:

- **Password reset activity**   This report provides a detailed view of password resets that occur in your organization.

- **Password reset registration activity**   This report provides a detailed view of password reset registration activities that occur in your organization.

- **Groups activity**   This report provides an activity log to view all group related activity occurring in your Azure AD directory.

> **TIP**   These reports can be scoped to a certain date range by using the provided date picker for both the start and end dates that you are interested in.

Integrated applications

These Azure AD Premium reports provide details about how cloud applications are being used and include:

- **Application usage**   This report provides a usage summary for all SaaS applications that have been integrated with your Azure AD directory.

> **TIP**   You can scope the interval for this report to the last twenty-four hours, seven days, or thirty days.

Azure Multi-Factor Authentication

Azure Multi-Factor Authentication capabilities are also included with Azure AD Premium and can help you secure access to your data and applications both in the cloud and on-premises applications made available for Azure AD authentication through VPN, RADIUS, and other forms of authentication. Multi-Factor Authentication (MFA), sometimes referred to as two-factor authentication, is a security best practice that requires that you identify yourself with more than just a password to access resources.

You can use MFA for all of your users to enforce stronger security measures or apply MFA policies to only selected users. For example, if you are unsure if a user account has been compromised, or if you think a user might be acting suspiciously, you can use Azure Multi-Factor Authentication to require that account to take additional verification steps that are beyond just entering a password. Azure Multi-Factor Authentication can request additional forms of verification through a mobile phone call, a mobile phone text message, or an office phone call. Alternatively, you could also provide a one-time password or use a push notification to a mobile device app to enable supplementary identity verification before allowing access to your apps and resources. Once you verify that the account has not been compromised, you can always easily disable MFA for the account.

The mobile device app helps secure access by providing an MFA option for verifying account sign-ins. The app, formerly named PhoneFactor, is now named *Multi-Factor Auth* in the Microsoft Store and *Multi-Factor Authentication* in the Google Play and Apple App stores. It can be downloaded and installed for free. Once installed, the Multi-Factor Auth app will notify you of a pending verification request by pushing an alert to your mobile device. When you receive the alert, you just need to view the request and then verify or cancel the MFA request. You could also be prompted by an application you are accessing to enter a passcode received by the Multi-Factor Auth app.

Getting the right Azure Multi-Factor Authentication app for your device

To use Azure Multi-Factor Authentication, simply install the free app on your mobile device. Be sure that the application you install includes the logo shown in Figure 3-2; those apps are the only ones supported for Azure Multi-Factor Authentication.

FIGURE 3-2   The Multi-Factor Auth app icon as seen in the app stores

You can use one of the following links to get the appropriate app for your device type:

- **Windows Phone**   *http://www.windowsphone.com/en-us/store/app/ phonefactor/0a9691de-c0a1-44ee-ab96-6807f8322bd1*
- **Android**   *https://play.google.com/store/apps/details?id=com.phonefactor.phonefactor*
- **iOS**   *https://itunes.apple.com/us/app/phonefactor/id475844606?mt=8*

After you install the app, you will receive instructions, which contain either an activation code and URL or a QR code, from the company that has enabled MFA for your account. Enter this information into the app or scan the QR code. You can activate multiple companies and accounts.

> **IMPORTANT**   The Multi-Factor Auth app requires connectivity to an active Azure Multi-Factor Authentication service and will not work without it.

User self-service from the Azure Access Panel

Users can easily access these self-service features as well as published applications from the Microsoft Azure Access Panel[3]. These Azure AD Premium features allow you to empower your end-users to be productive and get things done without having to call the helpdesk or becoming ensnared in time-consuming processes. There are several advantages to enabling self-service features made possible by Azure AD Premium, including:

- Your users can get access to published SaaS applications integrated with your Azure AD.
- Users can change and reset their own passwords or update their profiles to add missing information or to correct errors.
- IT can easily assign groups to SaaS apps to grant access and users can create and manage their own groups from the Azure Access Panel. From there, group owners can easily access and manage group membership requests.

> **TIP** By using the Configure tab for your directory in the Azure Account portal[4], you can customize the Access Panel to brand it with your company logo, pictures, and color schemes to provide a consistent look and feel for your organization across websites and services.

SaaS application availability

Your users can access SaaS applications that you integrate with Azure AD simply and quickly just by logging in to the Azure Access Panel. You can publish applications that you develop yourself or simply add an application from the gallery. Currently there are more than 3,000 SaaS applications available from within the Azure application gallery to integrate with your Azure AD domain.

Once you integrate a SaaS application with your directory, you can control access to the app using self-service group management. You can do that by assigning one or more security groups to manage access from the application properties on the Users And Groups tab of the application properties, as shown in Figure 3-3.

---

[3] The Azure Access Panel is available at *https://myapps.microsoft.com*.

[4] You can learn more about applying company branding to the Azure Access Panel page at *http://msdn.microsoft.com/library/azure/dn532270.aspx#bkmk_customizable*.

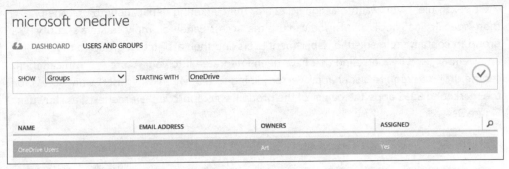

FIGURE 3-3 Controlling access to SaaS apps by assigning one or more security groups in the application properties

To make it even easier to use SaaS applications, when you integrate them with your Azure AD, you have the option of allowing all group members to authenticate to the SaaS application from within the Access Panel using stored credentials. This can be useful if you have a centralized SaaS app account used by more than one person in the organization, such as a company Facebook or Twitter account. Alternatively, you can enable Single Sign-On (SSO) for apps in order to require users to authenticate using their organizational credentials. If you are curious if a particular app is used often, you can easily see usage reports on the Dashboard tab of the application properties.

As you will learn in the next chapter, SaaS apps that support federation with Azure AD, such as Google Apps, Box, Office 365 and others, can be signed in to from the Access Panel using just about any web browser that supports JavaScript and cascading style sheets without requiring a web browser plug-in or mobile app. However, for users to sign in to apps that are configured to use password-based SSO, an Access Panel web browser extension is required to be installed and enabled. The extension is downloaded automatically when a user tries to access an application that is configured for password-based SSO.[5] To access password-based SSO apps using iOS or Android devices, users need to install the My Apps mobile app published by the Azure AD team and made available in both the Google Play store and the Apple App store.[6]

Self-service group management

It is easy for users to create and manage security groups that enable access to SaaS applications integrated with Azure AD. Requests to join groups can either be auto-approved or they can require the owner of the group to approve or deny the request. This saves you a lot of time and hassle because you no longer need to manually administer user-access rights to every SaaS application in use.

---

[5] The Access Panel web browser extension is currently supported on IE 8 and later, Chrome, and Firefox browsers.

[6] The My Apps mobile app is currently supported on Android 4.1 and up and iOS 7 and up on iPad and iPhone.

For example, if you want to assign access for the marketing department to use one or more specific SaaS applications, you can use the Access Panel to simply create a security group to contain the marketing department users and then assign that group to the SaaS applications used by marketing that have been integrated into your Azure AD. You can then set the group to require owner approval for joining so that when other users want access to the marketing SaaS apps, the owner of the group has to approve their requests, as shown in Figure 3-4.

FIGURE 3-4   The security group membership request Approvals user interface in the Azure Access Panel as seen by the group owner

By managing access to the SaaS applications used by the marketing department this way, you save time and users get access to the apps they need to get their jobs done more quickly. When a user is added to the group, that user immediately receives the apps assigned to the security group; those apps are automatically removed from the user's list of applications in the Access Panel when the user leaves the Marketing group.

> **TIP**   Do you think you don't have any SaaS applications to manage in your enterprise? Run the Azure AD Cloud App Discovery (*http://appdiscovery.azure.com/*) and find out. Most enterprises discover many more SaaS applications in use than they would have guessed.

Self-service password management

In addition to applications and group management, your users can also use the Azure Access Panel to manage their profile information and passwords themselves as shown in Figure 3-5.

The self-service change password functionality allows your users to simply log on to the Access Panel to change their passwords without needing to call the helpdesk. If a user cannot remember his password, then he can also use password reset to obtain a new password. Changing a password is a very simple process, but before users can reset their passwords, they must first have at least one multifactor authentication method defined from the following options: office phone, mobile phone, or alternate email address.

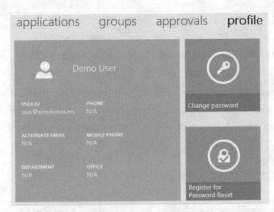

FIGURE 3-5 Azure AD Premium self-service options for group management and password reset

The ability to reset and change user passwords is enabled by default for user accounts created in Azure, but to enable passwords to be changed for user accounts synchronized to your Azure AD from on-premises Active Directory, you must enable the Password Write Back option when configuring directory synchronization. This option provides a cloud-based option for your users to reset their on-premises passwords wherever they are located while still enforcing on-premises password complexity rules and without opening any inbound firewall ports.

Understanding directory integration

Of course, before you can use Azure AD Premium features that depend on user cloud identities for authentication, you need to have some users in your Azure AD! Accordingly, directory integration is really all about creating an identity bridge between on-premises and Azure AD to manage identities, users, and groups, as well as manage access to applications though a central Azure AD management console. Most enterprises have made a significant investment in their on-premises Active Directory and do not want to have to manually re-create every single user and group object in Azure AD. By integrating your on-premises Active Directory with Azure AD, you can extend identity to the cloud and leverage all the hard work you've done to manage your users, groups, and on-premises resource access controls.

> **TIP** The centralized identity management and access solution created by combining on-premises Active Directory and the cloud-based Azure AD is the key to enabling your users to work anywhere from any device.

Synchronizing your on-premises Active Directory objects with Azure AD enables users to sign in to cloud-based services using a single identity based on the same usernames and passwords they already use to access local resources on-premises. Taking it a step further, you can federate an on-premises domain with the custom domain that is registered and verified for use with the Azure AD to enable true SSO. Using that single identity, you can then centrally manage access to Microsoft Online Services such as Azure, Office 365, Dynamics CRM Online, Microsoft Intune, and many other Microsoft and non-Microsoft cloud applications.

The remainder of this section describes several key aspects of directory integration that you should understand and consider before implementing your own plans for on-premises to Azure AD integration. This will help you decide whether or not you want to synchronize your directories, federate your domains, or both.

Source of authority

When you create users or other objects in Azure AD by using either a Windows PowerShell cmdlet or account portal tools such as the Microsoft Intune or Office 365 admin portals, those objects are considered "mastered" in the cloud. Because these mastered objects were created in the cloud, they can only be modified via cloud-based directory tools. This is referred to as the *source of authority* and there can only be one source of authority for each object in Azure AD to prevent data loss. So, in the example just given, the cloud-based directory would be authoritative over those objects for future changes.

Once you activate and start synchronizing your on-premises Active Directory information to Azure AD, the source of authority will be transferred to the on-premises Active Directory immediately after the first sync cycle completes. When that change is complete, the Azure AD user and group objects belonging to your on-premises domain will become read-only in the Azure AD management portal. That being the case, after the source of authority has changed to your local Active Directory, you will be powerless to modify them from the Azure portal and you must create or modify users using your on-premises tools if you want them synchronized with Azure AD. This change has no effect on objects that were created in the cloud because they are not linked to objects in your on-premises Active Directory.

> **IMPORTANT** After the first successful directory synchronization, you can only update synchronized directory objects stored in the cloud from your on-premises environment.

Directory synchronization

An easy way to understand how directory synchronization works is shown in Figure 3-6, where you can think of it as a kind of simple extension cord linking your on-premises users to the cloud and "lighting up" cloud-based services and application identity and access management scenarios.

FIGURE 3-6 Directory synchronization is like powering up Azure to turn on application access

The goal of directory synchronization is to create a single identity for each user that identifies them both on-premises and in the cloud. This identity synchronization is accomplished by linking what is basically a copy of your on-premises Active Directory user and group accounts in Azure AD. Once activated, directory synchronization occurs on a regular schedule about every three hours and is meant to ensure that any ongoing changes occurring in your on-premises directories are accurate and automatically reflected in Azure AD. The automated process helps to reduce administrative costs by leveraging your existing on-premises user and group accounts so that you do not have to manually re-create them in Azure AD. It also reduces the amount of time necessary to enable access to cloud-based services for your users and increases security to shared resources and apps by automatically keeping synchronized group memberships updated.

> **TIP** Directory synchronization also allows global address list (GAL) synchronization if you want to integrate an on-premises Microsoft Exchange Server environment with Microsoft Exchange Online.

Directory synchronization can be turned on and off as needed and here are three ways to do it that from your Azure AD's Directory Integration tab in the Azure portal:

- **Activate** Activating directory synchronization from the Microsoft Azure account portal is required to start the flow of on-premises object attributes to Azure AD. Remember that after the first synchronization is complete, the source of authority for everything stored in the cloud that corresponds to something in the local Active Directory will be set to the on-premises directory.

- **Deactivate** Deactivating directory synchronization from the Azure account portal stops the transfer of on-premises object attributes to Azure AD. When this happens, the source of authority is transferred from the on-premises directory to the cloud-based Azure AD. You should do this only when you no longer want or need to manage objects from on-premises.

- **Reactivate** If you change your mind and decide to return the source of authority for directory objects to on-premises, you can do that by reactivating directory synchronization. Be careful when doing this; reactivating directory synchronization in this manner could lead to data loss. For example, if objects have been created or modified in the cloud since they were last uploaded by the local directory sync, then those changes would immediately be lost because the synchronization process would instantaneously begin overwriting object data from on-premises back to the cloud.

When you synchronize your local on-premises Active Directory objects and their associated password hashes with Azure AD, you enable your users to be authenticated by Azure AD using their on-premises credentials. The basic architecture behind directory synchronization is shown in Figure 3-7. It shows the one-way transfer of object data from the on-premises Active Directory through the directory sync tool and to the Azure AD directory with directory sync activated. In this configuration, your on-premises objects and attributes will be synchronized and made available for identity and resource access management in the cloud.

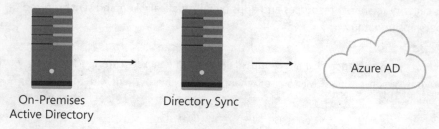

On-Premises   Directory Sync
Active Directory

FIGURE 3-7 Synchronizing on-premises Active Directory with Azure AD

Active Directory Federation Services

As you have seen, you do not necessarily have to federate domains in order to enable your users to authenticate in to Azure AD with the same usernames and passwords that they use on-premises. There are certainly situations in which directory sync capabilities alone will meet your organizational needs, but eventually you will need more than just basic authentication enabled by directory synchronization. Extending your authentication capabilities to provide a single, federated identity for each user enables you to better deliver a seamless user experience through Active Directory Federation Services (AD FS) and SSO.

Figure 3-8 shows the more complex identity and authentication scenario involving SSO via AD FS to enable on-premises authentication. Notice that you must still use identity synchronization tools to populate your Azure AD with on-premises objects, but now authentication to cloud-based services is handled by your on-premises Windows Server Active Directory rather than Azure AD.

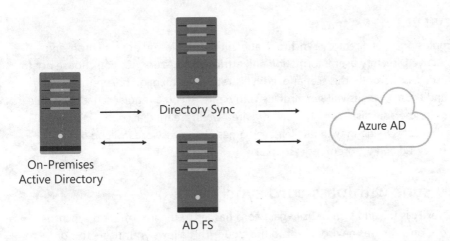

On-Premises Active Directory

Directory Sync

Azure AD

AD FS

FIGURE 3-8 Synchronizing on-premises Active Directory with Azure AD to enable SSO using on-premises authentication enabled by AD FS

Before you begin using SSO, you will need to add your organization's public domain name to your Azure AD instance and then verify it for directory integration in the Azure management portal. When that is completed, you will need to prepare your on-premises domain to configure certain settings to work properly with SSO. In particular, the user principal name (UPN), also known as a user logon name, must be set up in a specific way for each user to match the domain that you have added and verified in Azure AD for directory synchronization.

The following are important points to consider when preparing your on-premises Active Directory for directory synchronization with Azure AD:

- The domain you choose to federate must be registered as a public domain.
- The UPN added to users to be synchronized with Azure AD and for SSO can only contain letters, numbers, periods, dashes, and underscores.
- The UPN domain suffix must be added under the domain that you choose to set up for SSO and known by your users.

Directory integration scenarios

Now that you understand how directory integration works, you are ready to learn more about the various synchronization options available to you by using the different identity synchronization tools that are available.

Depending on your organization's needs and policies, directory synchronization can be done a few different ways. Starting simple, you can go from a basic synchronization of user and group attributes only (without passwords) all the way to synchronizing on-premises objects and password hashes from multiple forests to Azure AD.

Directory sync

This is the simplest form of directory synchronization in that while you are synchronizing on-premises Active Directory user information and attributes to Azure AD, you choose not to synchronize user passwords. In this scenario, administrators can manage on-premises directory objects and those changes will synchronize with Azure AD on a regular schedule. While this does alleviate the administrator overhead required when creating accounts in Azure AD, and it will enable users to log in with familiar usernames, their passwords will be different when accessing cloud and on-premises resources.

Directory sync with password sync

Next in complexity is the addition of user-password hashes to the information synchronized from your on-premises environment to the cloud. This allows your users to sign in to Azure AD and other cloud services (such as Office 365 or Microsoft Intune) using the same user names and passwords that they use on-premises. This means that user authentication can occur in both locations and that the passwords are always the same as long as the synchronization of on-premises data occurs on schedule. Having the same password in both locations provides *same sign-on* for users because they can now use the same usernames and passwords when authenticating to both on-premises and cloud-based resources and applications.

When using password sync[7], the plain-text version of a user's password is not synchronized to Azure AD or any other cloud service. Instead, the user password information that is synchronized from the on-premises Active Directory is the stored hash value representations of the actual user passwords. The password hash synchronized to Azure AD cannot be used to log in to on-premises networks and it also cannot be reversed in an effort to discover the user's plaintext password.

> **IMPORTANT** On-premises Active Directory directories that are configured for Federal Information Processing Standards (FIPS)[8] are not compatible with password sync.

Directory sync with SSO

This synchronization method is used to provide users with seamless login experiences as they can access cloud services while logged on with their corporate network credentials. However, in order to set up SSO, you have to first deploy a security token service on-premises, such as

---

[7] You can read more about password synchronization at *http://msdn.microsoft.com/en-us/library/azure/dn246918.aspx*.

[8] You can learn more about FIPS at *http://www.nist.gov/itl/fipsinfo.cfm*.

AD FS. That on-premises service then authenticates users coming in from the cloud based on their on-premises identity attributes. Once set up, users can simply use their existing on-premises company sign-on information to access both the services in the cloud as well as their existing on-premises resources.

Multiforest directory sync with SSO

This is the most complex directory synchronization scenario. It is basically the same as the single directory sync with SSO scenario described previously except there are multiple on-premises directories configured to synchronize with Azure AD. Again, you have to deploy AD FS on-premises, but this is the best way to enable a seamless authentication experience from multiple forests with your cloud-based services and applications.

Directory synchronization tools

Once you have selected the synchronization strategy you want to implement, the next step is to choose the synchronization tool to use to get the job done. Several tools have been made available online from Microsoft to configure directory integration between your on-premises environment and Azure AD. The following three tools will be described, providing you with insight into how the tools evolved and clarifying any confusion about when to use each tool:

- Azure Active Directory Sync (DirSync)
- Azure Active Directory Synchronization Services (AAD Sync)
- Azure AD Connect

Based solely on the names of the synchronization tools you can probably understand how a lot of people get confused about which one to use. When you add in AD FS and SSO, things really get complicated. Luckily, Microsoft has heard that feedback and made vast improvements based on it in each subsequent synchronization tool release as you will see in the remainder of this section.

Azure Active Directory Synchronization Tool

Previously known as the Microsoft Online Services Directory Synchronization tool, Azure Active Directory Synchronization Tool (DirSync) is the first as well as the oldest tool you will look at in this section. It's so old, in fact, that it has basically been retired from active use and replaced by the Azure Active Directory Synchronization Services (AAD Sync) tool that will be covered next. However, for the sake of completeness and in an attempt to clarify the various directory sync tools available, it will be briefly touched on here. You can see the DirSync Welcome page in Figure 3-9.

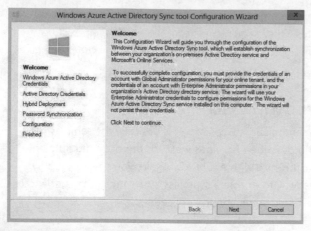

FIGURE 3-9 The Welcome page of the Windows Azure Active Directory Sync Tool Configuration Wizard

> **NOTE** If you already have DirSync functioning in your environment and it is doing everything you need it to do, there is no need to change synchronization tools. However, if you want to change tools, your best bet is to simply uninstall it and then install Azure AD Connect on the DirSync computer.

DirSync is a very basic application meant to simply provide a one-way synchronization from an organization's on-premises Active Directory to Azure AD on a schedule of about once every three hours. As is the case with all of the synchronization tools to be discussed, an administrator should install this tool and run it on only one computer in your organization's local network.

When you install DirSync, a service account is created in your Active Directory forest named something like MSOL_AD_SYNC or AAD_*xxxxxxxxxxxx* (with the 12 *x* characters replaced with some alphanumeric string representing your specific installation). You should not move, remove, or re-permission this service account or you will most likely cause synchronization failures.

As compared to the other two directory synchronization tools to be discussed, DirSync has several limitations, including the following:

- It can connect to only a single Active Directory forest (perhaps its most egregious limitation).

- It doesn't support the newer Azure AD Premium features, such as password change and password reset to Active Directory on-premises accounts.

- It does not allow advanced object attribute filtering.

Again, DirSync is basically obsolete at this point, but you are probably sure to come across it if you are searching online for Active Directory synchronization information. Time to move on to the newer directory synchronization tools.

Azure Active Directory Synchronization Services

Azure Active Directory Synchronization Services (Azure AD Sync) is relatively new and includes some major improvements over its DirSync predecessor. It supports Azure AD Premium features and is a step up from DirSync for more advanced configurations. The Azure AD Sync Welcome page is shown in Figure 3-10.

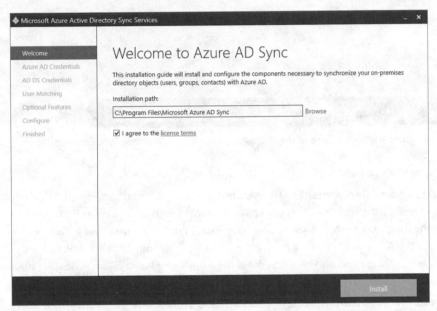

FIGURE 3-10 The Welcome page of the Azure Active Directory Sync Services Wizard

This synchronization service allows you to do the following:

- Synchronize single or multiforest Active Directory environments with Azure AD
- Configure advanced provisioning, mapping and filtering rules for objects and attributes, including support for syncing a very minimal set of user attributes
- Configure multiple on-premises Exchange organizations to map to a single AAD tenant.

In addition to synchronizing users and groups with Azure AD, Azure AD Sync also has optional features that allow you to enable enhanced functionality, as shown in Figure 3-11.

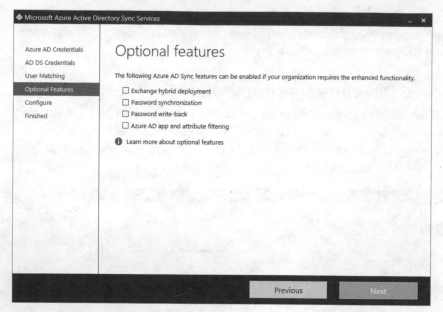

FIGURE 3-11 The Optional Features page of the Microsoft Azure Active Directory Sync Services Wizard

The optional features are as follows:

- **Exchange Hybrid Deployment**   Use this option when you need to support a unified email experience for a mix of users who have mailboxes with on-premises Exchange Server environments as well as users who have Exchange Online mailboxes. This feature of the Azure AD Sync tool enables users to find one another in the global address list (GAL) to send and receive emails regardless of which system is hosting their mailbox.

- **Password Synchronization**   Enable this feature to synchronize passwords from your on-premises Active Directory to Azure AD. When you enable password synchronization between your on-premises Active Directory and Azure AD, you need to grant the following permissions to the account that is used by Azure AD Sync to connect to your on-premises Active Directory to read password hash information: Replicating Directory Changes and Replicating Directory Changes All.

- **Password Write-Back**   Select this option to enable self-service functionality for users to reset their passwords from the Azure Access Panel. When this feature is enabled, Azure AD will synchronize the changes back to your on-premises Active Directory.

- **Azure AD App And Attribute Filtering**   This optional feature should be selected when you want to review or limit the attributes that are synchronized with Azure AD.

Just like DirSync, Azure AD Sync also configures directory sync to occur every three hours. However, there are ways to change the default schedule or to manually force a directory synchronization; these will be discussed in the next chapter. Directory synchronization is kept on schedule by a scheduled task running as the service account created when installing Azure

AD Sync on the directory synchronization server computer. An initial synchronization task will be run at the end of Azure AD Sync installation unless you cleared the option to run the initial synchronization in the installation wizard.

> **IMPORTANT** When you clear the check box for the option to synchronize changes during Azure AD Sync installation, the task will be installed as Disabled. After you configure the sync options according to your preferences, you need to Enable this scheduled task.

By default, the directory synchronization process will synchronize all of your on-premises users and groups to Azure AD. However, in most cases, you won't want to synchronize every single object from your on-premises Active Directory to Azure AD. Instead, you can use one of the following options to configure Active Directory synchronization filtering[9] to better scope the synchronization process to only what you need to be available in Azure AD:

- **Organizational unit** Select which OUs are allowed to sync with the cloud
- **Domain name** Define which OUs are allowed to sync with the cloud
- **User attributes** Specify user attributes to control which user objects should not be synchronized with Azure AD

> **TIP** If you accidentally synchronize more than you wanted to from your local Active Directory to Azure AD, don't worry. Just configure directory synchronization filtering and the objects that are filtered out from the next synchronization process will be removed from Azure AD.

Both of the directory synchronization tools that have been discussed thus far can be used to provision your Azure AD with on-premises user and group information, but neither will enable SSO or configure AD FS for you. If you are looking for a more complete directory synchronization tool that guides you through the complex configuration necessary to enable AD FS and SSO, then read on to discover the final—and recommended—directory synchronization tool that is used to complete the identity bridge from on-premises Active Directory to Azure AD.

Azure AD Connect

Making what used to be a very complicated and time consuming experience almost an afterthought because it is so easy now, the Microsoft Azure Active Directory Connect (AD Connect) Wizard provides a guided experience for integrating your on-premises Active Directory with Azure AD. It can be used to connect multiple Active Directory directories and

---

[9] You can learn more about Azure AD Sync filtering at *http://msdn.microsoft.com/ library/azure/dn801051.aspx.*

forests, will optionally guide you through the steps necessary to configure AD FS for SSO, and even finishes by verifying that the integration is successful. The Asure AD Connect Getting Started page is shown in Figure 3-12. (At the time of this writing, the Azure AD Connect Wizard was in Beta preview. The user interface might look a little different when you use it post-final release.)

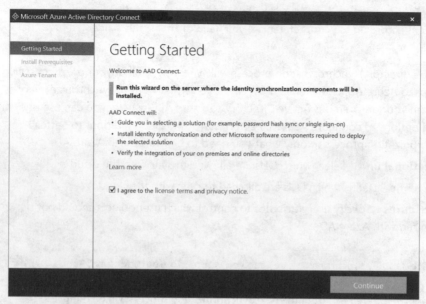

FIGURE 3-12   The Getting Started page of the Azure AD Connect Wizard

Azure AD Connect downloads, installs, and configures the identity bridge components for you that are necessary to configure a single, simple connection to Azure AD without requiring you to review pages and pages of documentation or download several tools. When you use this all-in-one tool for directory synchronization Azure AD Connect will:

- Download and install pre-requisites like the .NET Framework, Azure AD PowerShell Module, and Microsoft Online Services Sign-In Assistant.

- Azure AD connect will download and install all of the components necessary to configure and activate directory synchronization with your Azure AD directory. Configure either the password sync or the single sign-on option, depending on whether or not you select express settings or choose to use custom settings.

Azure AD Connect express settings

If you select to use express settings when installing Azure AD Connect to enable synchronization for a single Windows Server Active Directory forest, the wizard will automatically install AAD Sync on the server the wizard is installed on, configure synchronization of the on-premises Active Directory forest, enable password sync, and finally start the initial synchronization for you.

Azure AD Connect makes directory synchronization with the password sync for a single forest about as easy as can be imagined. After you download and start the wizard, it will set up everything for you with just a few mouse clicks, allowing sign-on to cloud resources based on Active Directory passwords with only a few minutes of work.

Azure AD Connect custom settings

If you want to go beyond basic directory and password synchronization, you can select to use custom settings when installing Azure AD Connect. In addition to directory synchronization, this option will guide you through the steps necessary to implement and configure AD FS for SSO.

You do not need to be an AD FS expert to configure SSO using Azure AD Connect because the wizard will guide you through each step of the process. However, you do need to have one SSL certificate[10] for your federation service name before you get started. That .pfx file will be imported and configured for you later on, when the wizard is configuring AD FS for you. AD FS and SSO really cannot get much easier.

Download Azure AD Connect

While this is the third directory synchronization tool discussed thus far, it is also the first synchronization tool to be recommended for you to download. Azure AD Connect is the simplest, most complete option for enabling both directory synchronization and identity federation.

This is the one directory synchronization tool that you want to be sure to have in your toolbox before continuing and you can get it at *http://aka.ms/dpzn0e*.

---

[10] You can learn more about the SSL certificate requirements to enable AD FS using Azure AD Connect at *http://msdn.microsoft.com/en-us/library/azure/dn832693.aspx*.

Chapter 4

Implementing hybrid identity

In Chapter 3, you learned about hybrid identity and how it enables users be productive on the devices they love while at the same time enabling IT to manage access to corporate resources and help keep company data secure in a cloud-first, mobile-first world.

In this chapter, you will take on the role of the senior enterprise administrator for the IT department at Blue Yonder Airlines and implement hybrid identity as the first phase of their EMS implementation plan as described at the end of Chapter 2. You will be responsible for ensuring Blue Yonder Airlines employees have a seamless Single Sign-On (SSO) experience and a consistent look and feel across all company websites and services both on the intranet and Internet.

Scenario description

As the senior enterprise administrator for Blue Yonder Airlines, you are responsible for planning, designing, and implementing the company's EMS solution. You know that hybrid identity is the key enabler to allowing your users to work from anywhere on any device, so you will start there.

Because you are already heavily invested in on-premises Windows Server 2012 Active Directory, which currently authenticates hundreds of users every day, you need to find a way to easily integrate that existing infrastructure with Microsoft Azure AD to leverage your on-premises investment. You also know that you will need to implement EMS with as little administrative overhead as possible while still enabling centralized reporting to monitor organizational activity and services.

Implementation goals

In addition to integrating the on-premises Active Directory with Azure AD, you will need to meet the following goals during the first phase of the EMS implementation plan for Blue Yonder Airlines:

- Leverage on-premises investment in Windows Server Active Directory and Microsoft Azure to deliver a hybrid identity solution that enables users to be productive while leaving IT in control.

- Implement SSO so that your users need only one name and one password to access both on-premises and cloud-based software and services.

- Enable a seamless transition user experience from on-premises to the cloud by providing a consistent look and feel across all managed websites and services.

Solution diagram

To meet the EMS implementation goals for the first phase of the project, you will need to implement the solution shown in Figure 4-1.

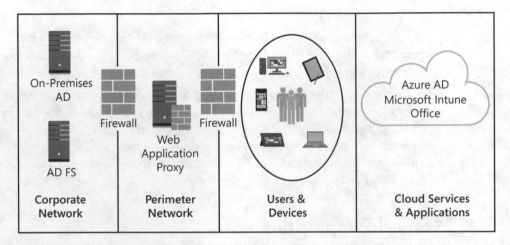

FIGURE 4-1 Hybrid identity enables users to access applications and cloud services from their devices while being authenticated by on-premises AD FS for SSO

> **TIP** This solution diagram is meant to provide a high-level overview and basic description of the intended solution architecture. Planning and design considerations for each element of the solution will be described in the next section.

The pieces of the solution diagram are:

- **Corporate network**   The corporate network, *corp.blueyonderairlines.com*, is where the on-premises Windows Server 2012 R2 Active Directory resides and where you will need to implement AD FS 3.0 to perform on-premises authentication for your users.

- **Perimeter network**   The perimeter network, or demilitarized zone or DMZ as it is sometimes called, is where you will install the Web Application Proxy as part of your AD FS 3.0 implementation.

- **Users and devices**   This part of the solution diagram represents the Blue Yonder Airlines employees and the devices they use on a regular basis—both company-owned and employee-owned.

- **Cloud services and applications**   This section represents the cloud services and Software-as-a-Service (SaaS) applications that Blue Yonder Airlines employee access from their devices.

Planning and designing the solution

Now that you have seen the completed solution picture from 10,000 feet, it is time to descend much lower into the individual technology and configuration requirements necessary to complete phase 1 of the EMS implementation plan. You will need to completely understand the information in this section to plan and prepare for the configuration steps necessary to successfully complete this phase of the project.

> **TIP**   This planning and design section is meant to provide you with additional details about the components and considerations to consider while implementing the hybrid identity solution. The next section will guide you through the actual implementation steps and show you what each of the components looks like in more detail.

Microsoft Azure planning and design considerations

As already discussed in chapter 3, Azure AD is a cloud-based service that provides identity and access management capabilities for Microsoft Azure resources as well as all Microsoft cloud services such as Microsoft Intune and Office 365. Azure AD is the key to extending your on-premises AD to the cloud and you will not be able to utilize EMS to its fullest extent until you synchronize on-premises user objects with your Azure AD service.

> **TIP**   A default Azure AD domain ends with *.onmicrosoft.com*. You will need to have global administrator credentials for your organization's default Azure AD domain to integrate it with your on-premises AD.

Microsoft Azure Management Portal

The Microsoft Azure Management Portal is used to manage your organization's directory data and to grant end-user access to resources managed by your Azure AD repository. As an administrator, you will have access to the Blue Yonder Airlines Azure AD tenant service that is associated with your subscription from within the Microsoft Azure Management Portal at *https://manage.windowsazure.com/* and as shown in Figure 4-2. From there, you can create and manage cloud-based users, groups, and SaaS applications, add custom domains, configure the Azure AD service itself, view reports, assign subscription licenses, and last, but not least, you can manage directory integration.

FIGURE 4-2 The Microsoft Azure Management Portal

> **TIP** As you plan for your Azure AD instance, you might need to consider how you will delegate administrative tasks to other administrators using the pre-defined Azure Management Portal administrative roles: billing administrator, global administrator, password administrator, service administrator, and user administrator. You can learn more about assigning Microsoft Azure administrative roles at *http://msdn.microsoft.com/en-us/library/azure/dn468213.aspx*.

Microsoft Azure Access Panel

Just like most organizations, Blue Yonder Airlines relies on many SaaS applications like Office 365, Box, and Salesforce for end-user productivity. When SaaS applications are published to Azure AD, they are integrated into the service which provides identity management and ease of access via the Microsoft Azure Access Panel and SSO for applications that are managed within your Azure AD service instance. In addition to the many SaaS applications available from the Azure application gallery, you can also integrate your on-premises web applications to allow Internet-based uses to access web applications hosted on-premises.

All of the configuration and integration is done in the Microsoft Azure Management Portal to make the entire process seamless to your users, who only need to go to *https://myapps.microsoft.com* and log on with their organizational account as shown in Figure 4-3.

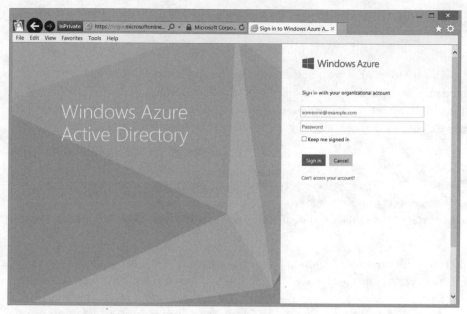

FIGURE 4-3 The Microsoft Azure AD sign-in page

After signing in to the Access Panel, users can also take advantage of the self-service functionality provided by Azure AD Premium features to perform password resets, update their profile information, perform password resets, or change their passwords without needing to call the helpdesk.

On-premises planning and design considerations

By definition, hybrid identity is all about getting your on-premises directory information into the cloud so that you can take advantage of Microsoft's enterprise-level cloud service features and functionality through integration with Azure AD. However, before you can successfully enable that integration, there are a few things that you will need to understand and configure.

The information in this section is critical to understanding how you will administer your Azure AD directory as well as how your users will sign into Microsoft cloud services. Be sure that you have a plan to completely address these considerations before attempting to integrate your directories.

User Principal Names

A user principal name (UPN) is an AD object attribute that provides an Internet-style sign-in name for a user account based on the Internet standard RFC 822. It is composed of the user's sign-in name and then the @ symbol followed by a UPN suffix. Shorter than a distinguished name, the UPN is easier to remember and usually maps to the user's email address.

By default, your users will have a domain UPN suffix based on the domain the account was created in. If multiple UPN suffixes are available, administrators can choose the default or alternative UPN to assign the user account from a drop-down list on the account properties in the Active Directory Users And Computers Microsoft Management Console (MMC) console snap-in.

As you plan your directory integration from on-premises to Azure AD, you will need to decide on the UPN suffix that will be used for your users to log onto cloud services. You might also need to plan for coordinating with the Active Directory administrators to add the UPN suffix, to apply the UPN suffix to the user accounts that you want to synchronize, or both.

Scope of directory integration

By default, the domain synchronization tools we've discussed might synchronize more objects with Azure AD than you need or want them to. As stated in Chapter 3, you can always apply a synchronization filter to remove those objects from Azure AD the next time synchronization runs.

However, if you do not want all the default objects to be synchronized, you will need to consider how you will scope the objects to be synchronized with Azure AD and plan your filtering strategy accordingly.

Single Sign-On components and considerations

Another aspect of preparing your on-premises environment for integration with Azure AD and SSO is understanding the requirements to implement the on-premises server infrastructure to support AD FS in your environment.

Remember, the end goal of enabling SSO for your users is to simplify your cloud-based administrative work and provide a seamless sign-on experience for your users to get access to cloud-based applications and services. In the past, configuring SSO has been a very complicated and cumbersome process to implement, but as you will see, there have been vast improvements made recently in this area to greatly simplify the process of installing and configuring AD FS for SSO with Windows Server 2012 R2.

Active Directory Federation Services 3.0

Active Directory Federation Services (AD FS) is the key to providing identity federation and SSO capabilities for your end users to access applications with federation partner organizations or cloud-based services. AD FS 3.0 is included as a federation service role in Windows Server 2012 R2 that authenticates users and provides access to applications and resources. You do not even need to install IIS on the server computer now because AD FS 3.0 is built with all of the IIS component it needs to work. And, as you will see later in the "Customize branding" section at the end of this chapter, it is also easy to customize the AD FS logon page using Windows PowerShell.

You will need to install and configure one or more AD FS 3.0 servers on Windows Server 2012 R2 server computers in your on-premises environment to enable SSO. To run the service itself, you can either create a standard service account or, if you have at least one Windows Server 2012 or later domain controller in your environment, you can use a group managed service account.

> **TIP** You do not need to install or configure AD FS manually because the Azure AD Connect Wizard will do it for you as part of configuring directory integration.

Web Application Proxy

The Web Application Proxy is a new role for Windows Server 2012 R2. It replaces the AD FS Proxy in legacy versions of AD FS and includes additional features, such as allowing administrators to publish internal websites, pre-authenticate users with AD FS, or allow pass-through authentication. The Web Application Proxy also provides reverse proxy functionality to enable users on any device to access web applications inside your corporate network from the Internet. You will need to install and configure the AD FS Web Application Proxy server on a Windows Server 2012 R2 server computer in your on-premises environment as part of enabling SSO, but you cannot install it on the same server that is hosting the AD FS server role.

While you can install this role on a non-domain joined computer, if you want to use integrated Windows authentication for your web applications, you will need to install the Web Application Proxy on a domain-joined server computer. You will most likely want to do this in your perimeter network because Secure Sockets Layer (SSL) endpoint must be opened up to the Internet to enable SSO from outside the corporate network for sign-ins and web application authentication when you publish web applications originating from your internal network.

When an authentication request is received by the Web Application Proxy, it will direct the request to the AD FS server to complete the authorization process. You will need to create an A Host (not a CNAME) record in your on-premises DNS to enable devices connecting from the intranet to contact the Web Application Proxy at the federation service name as it is displayed on the SSL certificate. To enable devices connecting from the Internet to access the AD FS service, you will need to create a CNAME record in public DNS to direct Internet traffic to the Web Application Proxy.

> **TIP** You do not need to install or configure the AD FS Web Application Proxy manually because the Azure AD Connect Wizard will do it for you as part of configuring directory integration. Also remember that you cannot install the AD FS server role and the AD FS Web Application Proxy roles on the same computer.

AD FS sign-in page

When you try to sign in to cloud-based services with an organizational account that has been federated with Azure AD, you will be automatically redirected by the Web Application Proxy to the organizational AD FS server's sign-in page with your sign-in name pre-populated on the sign-in screen for you. You can see the default sign-in page experience shown in Figure 4-4 and you will learn how to customize it using Windows PowerShell later in the chapter.

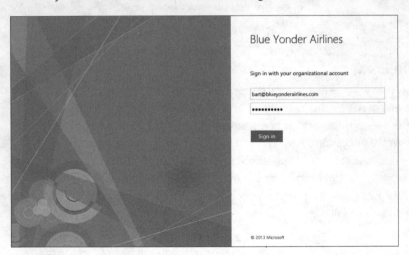

FIGURE 4-4 The default AD FS sign-in page

Certificate requirements

Security certificates are a vital component for safeguarding communication between AD FS and web-based devices and users and you will need to have a publicly trusted X509 v3 SSL certificate to secure your AD FS infrastructure. You can quickly and easily purchase the certificate from a public certificate authority company such as Verisign, DigiCert, or web-hosting companies like GoDaddy, but be sure that the subject name of the certificate to be used matches the federation service name that you will create in AD FS (something like adfs.blueyonderairlines.com).

MORE INFO You can learn more about the X509 public key certificates on MSDN at *http://msdn.microsoft.com/library/windows/desktop/bb540819(v=vs.85).aspx*.

You should use the same SSL certificate for both the AD FS server and the AD FS Web Application Proxy server computer. All client devices should also automatically trust the certificate because it was provided by a public certificate authority.

TIP You will need the certificate when you run the Azure AD Connect Wizard to configure AD FS and directory integration.

Azure AD Connect

The final on-premises planning consideration is the tool that will be used to enable domain integration from your Windows Server Active Directory to Azure AD. The wizard will handle all of the configuration and coordination necessary to get directory synchronization with Azure AD running as well as install AD FS and configure SSO for you. The Azure AD Connect Wizard provides a guided experience for:

- Downloading and installing integration component prerequisites for running the wizard, such as the .NET Framework, the Azure AD PowerShell Module, and the Microsoft Online Services Sign-In Assistant.

- Downloading, installing, and configuring Azure AD Sync and enabling directory sync in your Azure AD tenant service.

- Configuring either password sync or AD FS with Azure AD for you, depending on what option you choose to use.

- Validating that everything is working at the completion of the wizard.

- Even if you configure SSO, the Azure AD Connect Wizard will still give you the option to configure password hash sync to enable sign in using on-premises passwords as a fall back in case AD FS goes down.

The server computer that you run Azure AD Connect on will be used for managing the synchronization service with Azure AD. The identity synchronization components will be installed on this computer, but you can also make it an AD FS server. If you do not want the wizard to install AD FS on the synchronization computer, or if you want to install AD FS on additional computers to create an AD FS server farm, you can have the wizard install the AD FS and Web Application Proxy server roles on any other accessible Windows Server 2012 R2 server computers.

Azure AD Connect is a very powerful wizard that makes it extremely easy to quickly configure directory synchronization with Azure AD and enable SSO via AD FS for users in your environment, but it does require several items that you should plan for before you start it. In addition to having at least two Windows Server 2012 R2 server computers and the federation services SSL certificate (and certificate password) available, you will also need to have the following information on hand before running the Azure AD Connect Wizard:

- Azure AD global tenant admin credentials.

- On-premises Windows Server Active Directory enterprise administrator credentials.

- The FQDN for the server names on which you want to install AD FS. It can be the same server you run the wizard to install the synchronization engine on or one or more remote servers if you want to create an AD FS server farm.

- The FQDN for the server on which you want to install the Web Application Proxy.

- Domain credentials that the Web Application Proxy will use when requesting certificates from the AD FS server. This domain user account must be an administrator on the AD FS server.

- If you do not have a Windows Server 2012 domain controller in your environment you will need to create an AD FS service account. Otherwise, with a Windows Server 2012 domain controller in your environment, you can use a Group Managed Service account.

> **MORE INFO**   You can learn more about group managed service accounts on TechNet at *http://technet.microsoft.com/en-us/library/hh831782.aspx*.

- A public domain name that your company owns and that is already verified in Azure AD. If you have not previously verified the domain name in the Microsoft Azure Management Portal, you will be prompted to verify it by the wizard, but because it can take some time for that to happen you are better off pre-verifying the domain in Azure AD before running the wizard.

Real World   Identity and access management benefits of implementing hybrid identity

Extending your Windows Server Active Directory to Azure Active Directory enables new scenarios that will have a significant impact on your organization. You can now simplify access and control of both cloud and on-premises applications, reduce your IT burden with self-service identity and access management, improve security posture with anomaly reporting and multifactor authentication services, and easily meet both business and security reporting needs. These scenarios are enabled through capabilities available with Azure AD Premium, which is one of the key components of the Enterprise Mobility Suite.

Through Azure AD, you can now easily manage end user access to all the common SaaS applications, including Office 365, Workday, Salesforce, Yammer, and your existing on-premises applications. You gain Azure AD SSO for SaaS applications as well as your on-premises applications with the Azure AD application proxy, and automated user provisioning and de-provisioning to ServiceNow and other SaaS applications. End users accessing your services gain company-branded sign-in and user experience when accessing all of these applications.

To begin gaining control and enabling end user single sign on, many organizations need an inventory of cloud applications in use. Azure AD Premium provides a solution that includes an interactive dashboard displaying the total number of SaaS apps in use across the organization, the number of users using SaaS apps, and the top SaaS apps in use with rich reporting for administrator's review.

Self-service for the end user offers both security and productivity gains and enables the change and reset of end user passwords from the cloud and writing these passwords back to on-premises AD to support both cloud and on-premises resources. Self-service password management is supported through phone and email verification methods, end-user registration of their own contact information, and customized helpdesk URL and branding of the portal for resetting passwords.

Azure AD Premium offers a self-service group management solution that enables distributed group creation and management, and the ability for end-users to create groups and assign users to the groups. Group owners can delegate group ownership and users can search for groups and make requests to join.

Using Azure AD Premium, organizations can implement a range of security features, including machine learning that supports detecting access anomalies including credential sharing, credential misuse/loss and brute force attacks. IT administrators are notified when possible security issues are detected, and the administrator can investigate while downloading data as needed for offline analysis.

Organizations can also protect access to sensitive applications, while avoiding locking out end users by using several methods of Multi-Factor Authentications (MFA), such as a phone app, call or SMS mobile, office, or alternate phone. Organizations can use targeted MFA for sensitive accounts, end-user self-service enrollment and audit reports for MFA activity.

To begin gaining control and to enable single sign on, many organizations need an inventory of cloud applications in use. Azure AD Premium provides a solution that includes an interactive dashboard displaying total number of SaaS apps in use across the organization, the number of users using SaaS apps and the top SaaS apps in use with rich reporting for administrator's review.

We look forward to you experiencing these comprehensive identity and access management capabilities and giving us feedback on your experiences.

Keith Brintzenhofe
Group Program Manager, Microsoft Azure AD Identity and Access Management, Microsoft Corporation.

Implementing the hybrid identity solution

Now that you have an understanding of the components involved and you have completed the requisite pre-planning to ensure your success, the time has come for you to begin implementing the hybrid identity solution for Blue Yonder Airlines so that the company can begin utilizing EMS and fully enjoy the benefits it provides.

Prepare the Azure AD service for directory integration

To prepare the Azure AD service for directory integration with the Blue Yonder Airlines on-premises AD, you will first need to add and verify the *blueyonderairlines.com* public domain name and then activate domain synchronization from within the Microsoft Azure Management Portal.

Add and verify your public domain

The first step in preparing the Azure AD service for integration with the on-premises Blue Yonder Airlines AD is to add and verify ownership of the custom domain name. You know you can do this because your company owns the public domain name blueyonderairlines.com and you have the necessary credentials to ensure that the DNS records required to verify the domain can be modified with the domain name registrar.

Complete the following steps to successfully add and verify the custom domain:

1. Sign in to the Microsoft Azure Management Portal with global administrator credentials.

2. Open the Active Directory node of the Azure Management Portal.

3. Select the Azure AD instance to be modified.

4. On the Domains tab, select Add A Custom Domain and then click Add. You do not need to select the I Plan To Configure This Domain For Single Sign-On With My Local Active Directory check box because you will verify the domain next as part of this process rather than when configuring domain federation integration using Azure AD Connect.

5. After receiving the notification that the domain was successfully added, click the arrow to continue. Use the information displayed on the next page to go to your domain registrar and update the DNS settings for the custom domain to add the required TXT record to the applicable DNS zone. (You can learn more about verifying your domain name with a domain registrar on MSDN at *http://msdn.microsoft.com/library/azure/jj151803.aspx.)*

> **TIP** It can take anywhere from 15 minutes to 72 hours for the DNS zone changes to take effect before you can verify the domain, so it's a good idea to get this out of the way as soon as possible.

6. Back in the Microsoft Azure Management Portal, select the custom domain name on the Domains tab and then click the Verify button at the bottom of the page to open the domain verification dialog box.

7. Click the Verify button to verify the domain and close the dialog box. You should now see Verified for the custom domain status on the Domains tab as shown in Figure 4-5.

FIGURE 4-5 Custom domain added and verified in the Microsoft Azure Management Portal

Activate directory synchronization in Azure AD

Activating directory synchronization from the Microsoft Azure Management Portal is required to prepare the service to accept on-premises object attributes into your Azure AD service. The Azure AD Connect Wizard will do this for you if you forget, but it's best to go ahead and get it out of the way while you're still working in the portal.

Complete the following steps to activate directory integration for the Azure AD service:

1. Continuing in the Azure Management Portal, ensure your Azure AD service name is still selected and click the Directory Integration tab.

2. In the Integration With Local Activate Directory section, click Activated and then select Save at the bottom of the page.

3. Select Yes on the Activate Directory Sync dialog box.

4. Verify that you see the Changing Directory Integration Status message at the bottom of the portal. After a few minutes, the message should change to Successfully Changed The Directory Integration Status. Click OK and verify that the Directory Sync status is now Activated.

Prepare the on-premises environment for directory integration

After successfully preparing the Azure AD service for directory synchronization, you now need to focus on what needs to get done to prepare the on-premises environment.

As the enterprise admin for Blue Yonder Airlines you have permissions to make all of the necessary modifications, but don't forget that you still need to coordinate with the other domain administrators to ensure that they are all aware of the changes you will be making to the on-premises AD and DNS settings as well as why you are making them. The server team will also need to provide you with at least two Windows Server 2012 R2, domain-joined server computers with one configured for perimeter network access.

Add an alternate UPN suffix to support the public domain

The first thing that you need to do is add the custom domain name that will be federated with Azure AD to the domain suffix list in the on-premises AD.

To do that, you will need to follow these steps while logged on with your administrator credentials on a Windows Server 2012 Active Directory server:

1. Open Administrative Tools from the Start menu and then click Active Directory Domains And Trusts.

2. In the console tree, right-click Active Directory Domains And Trusts and then click Properties.

3. On the UPN Suffixes tab, add the alternative UPN suffix for the custom domain (in this case, *blueyonderairlines.com*) and then click Add, as shown in Figure 4-6.

4. Click OK to close the properties dialog box and exit the Active Directory Domains And Trusts console.

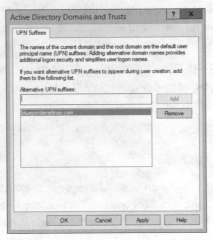

FIGURE 4-6 Adding the custom UPN suffix to the on-premises AD

Configure users and groups for synchronization

Because you do not want to immediately synchronize all users and groups with Azure AD, the first step you take to configure on-premises AD objects for synchronization should be to create a new organization unit (OU) in the on-premises AD. You will use that as a container to organize the specific users and groups that you want to sync with Azure AD as part of the pilot phase of implementing EMS at Blue Yonder Airlines.

After creating the OU, you need to add the users and groups that you want to sync with Azure AD. You will also need to configure the alternate UPN suffix for each user so that each user can use that federated sign-in name for cloud services authentication.

To add users to the Cloud Service Users OU, you will need to follow these steps while still logged on with your administrator credentials on a Windows Server 2012 Active Directory server:

1. Open Active Directory Users And Computers from Administrative Tools. Right-click the domain name (in this case, corp.blueyonderairlines.com) and then click New\Organizational Unit. Name the new OU Cloud Service Users and then click OK to close the New Object – Organizational Unit dialog box.

2. Next, you need to navigate through the existing OUs to move user accounts for those who will be part of the EMS pilot into the new Cloud Service Users OU. When you are finished, you should have an OU containing the users that will be synchronized, looking something like Figure 4-7.

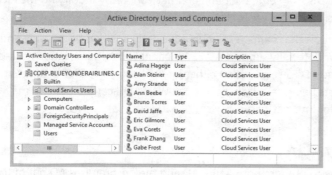

FIGURE 4-7 Custom OU populated with cloud service users to synchronize with Azure AD

3. Finally, you need to configure the UPN suffix for all of the pilot users in the Cloud Service Users OU so that they will be ready for SSO using the blueyonderairlines.com public domain name that you added to Azure AD. To do that, you simply select all of the user accounts in the Cloud Service Users OU, right-click one and select Properties. Next, select the Account tab and configure the appropriate UPN suffix from the drop-down list to bulk update all of the user accounts at once.

Configure name resolution

The final step in preparing the on-premises environment is to ensure that the necessary DNS settings have been configured properly. You need to enable the name resolution to support the AD FS functionality required for users connecting to published web applications from within the corporate network to authenticate into those apps as well as enable the Web Application Proxy server computer to resolve the AD FS server name to authenticate users signing in from outside the corporate network.

To allow intranet users to authenticate into web applications and resources using AD FS, you need to go into the on-premises DNS server and create an Host (A) record for the IP address of the AD FS server (or AD FS load-balancer if you are using an AD FS farm) that corresponds to the AD FS service you will create when you enable SSO. You know from your previous planning and from when you purchased the SSL certificate for Blue Yonder Airlines that you will name the service *adfs.blueyonderairlines.com*, so you add a Host record for that name in the DNS forward lookup zone for blueyonderairlines.com in the on-premises DNS.

Because the Web Application Proxy is actually the computer that users signing in from the Internet will need to contact to enable SSO authentication, you will need to ensure that port 443 is open to Internet communication on the Web Application Proxy and that the server can be contacted on an external network interface card configured with an Internet-accessible IP address. That IP address will need to be registered with your domain name registrar so that the host name matches the AD FS service name (in this case, adfs.blueyonderairlines.com). Finally, the Web Application Proxy must be able to resolve the internal AD FS server name by either using an alternate DNS server in the perimeter network or by modifying the local HOSTS file on the Web Application Server itself.

The end result of all of this is that name resolution is properly enabled both inside and outside the corporate network to fully support AD FS functionality. Authentication requests should now be routed to the AD FS server using either internal company DNS settings or from authentication requests being sent by proxy via the Web Application Proxy to the on-premises AD FS server for Internet-based devices.

Enable Single Sign-On

With all the hard work done to prepare both Azure AD and the on-premises AD out of the way, the only thing left to do is to enable SSO and verify that your pilot users appear in Azure AD. Luckily, the Azure AD Connect Wizard will do most of the work for you as long as you supply it with the public SSL certificate you purchased for the AD FS service name and have properly planned to provide the other information it needs to complete the job for you.

> **TIP** At the time of this writing, the Azure AD Connect Wizard was in Beta, so your experience might vary depending on any changes made to the Wizard at its final release.

Use the Azure AD Connect Wizard to configure domain synchronization, federate your domains, and configure AD FS to enable SSO by following these steps:

1. Download the latest version of Azure AD Connect from *http://aka.ms/aadconnect* on the Windows Server 2012 R2 computer that you will use for the synchronization computer.

2. Open MicrosoftAzureActiveDirectoryConnect.msi to start the Azure AD Connect Wizard. Once started, the wizard will check for installation prerequisites to determine

if prerequisites like Microsoft .NET Framework 3.5, Microsoft Online Services Sign-In Assistant For IT Professionals, Azure AD Sync Engine, or the Windows Azure Active Directory Module For Windows PowerShell need to be automatically downloaded and installed.

3. After installing the necessary prerequisites, the Azure AD Connect Wizard will prompt you for your Azure AD global administrator credentials. After your credentials are verified with Microsoft Online the wizard will proceed to the next step.

4. Next, you need to select the Active Directory forest that you want to synchronize with Azure AD. You only need to synchronize a single Active Directory forest, so you select that option and then select Single Sign On as the sign on experience you would like the wizard to configure for you, as shown in Figure 4-8.

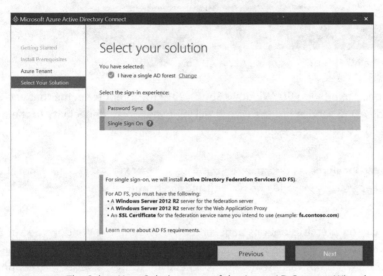

FIGURE 4-8 The Select Your Solution page of the Azure AD Connect Wizard

5. After verifying your Azure AD credentials and getting an understanding of what you want to do, the wizard will start the on-premises information gathering process by asking you to provide the enterprise administrator credentials for the on-premises Windows Server Active Directory.

6. On the AD FS Farm page of the Azure AD Connect Wizard you will be prompted to either create a new Windows Server 2012 R2 AD FS farm or use an existing one. For this scenario, select the option to deploy a new AD FS farm and then click Browse to select the SSL certificate (PFX file) that you purchased to use for the AD FS service certificate. You will most likely need to enter the password for the exported certificate, as shown in Figure 4-9. After it is imported, select the AD FS service name (in this case, adfs.blueyonderairlines.com) and then verify the federation service name is correct.

FIGURE 4-9 The AD FS Farm page of the Azure AD Connect Wizard

7. Next, you need to provide the Windows Server 2012 R2 computer name that you want to install the AD FS service on. The wizard will verify network connectivity to the server and then add it as a selected server.

> **TIP** You can add multiple server names on this page to create an AD FS server farm, but for this scenario you will just add one server name and continue.

8. On the specify on-premises options page, enter the name of the Windows Server 2012 R2 computer that you want the wizard to install the Web Application Proxy server role on. The wizard will again validate network connectivity to the server before continuing.

> **TIP** The Web Application Proxy cannot be installed on the same server as the AD FS service computer and it does not need to be domain-joined as it is often a standalone server in the perimeter network. However, to enable integrated Windows authentication to published web apps, you will use a domain-joined server in the perimeter network with a firewall rule that allows 443 traffic between the Web Application Proxy server and the AD FS server only.

9. On the Specify Federation Server Credentials page, you need to enter a username and password for the credentials that will be used by the Web Application Proxy to request a certificate from the federation server. This service account only needs to be a regular domain user account, but it must also be an administrator on the AD FS servers.

10. On the Specify Federation Service Account page you should select the Create A Group Managed Service Account (gMSA) For Me option because you know that Blue Yonder

Airlines on-premises AD has Windows Server 2012 domain controllers to support this type of account.

11. On the Specify Domain For Federation page, select the domain name that you want to federate from the drop-down list.

> **TIP** If you had not already previously verified the domain name, the wizard would have prompted you with information and directions for you to confirm you own the domain name before completing AD FS installation. If you continue without first verifying the domain name, the wizard will start the initial synchronization but will not create the AD FS trust with Azure AD. This is why you were proactive and have already verified the blueyonderairlines.com domain in Azure AD.

12. The Review Options page is displayed next and offers you the opportunity to review the settings that the wizard will execute when you click Install on this page. Because you do not want to synchronize all users and groups with Azure AD, you clear the Start Synchronization Process As Soon As The Initial Configuration Completes check box as shown in Figure 4-10, but you do leave the second check box selected to provide fallback authentication in case AD FS goes down for some reason in the future.

> **TIP** After you click Install on this page, the Wizard will begin installing and configuring identity synchronization components and AD FS in your environment. The process will take about half an hour as the wizard downloads and installs components necessary to enable directory sync and install and configure AD FS for you.

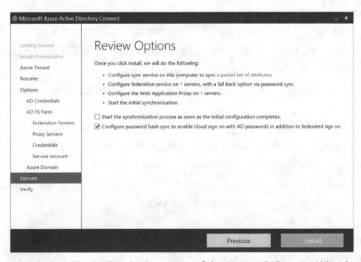

FIGURE 4-10 The Review Options page of the Azure AD Connect Wizard

13. When the installation is complete, the wizard gives you the option to verify that the DNS name resolution that you configured earlier is functioning properly by clicking the Verify button or you can just exit the wizard. Because you want to be sure everything is working properly, click Verify to continue.

14. Finally, the Wizard will verify both the intranet and extranet configuration and the IP addresses that the federation service name responds to on both internal and external DNS Servers and you can exit the wizard.

Configure synchronization filtering

After successfully completing the Azure AD Connect Wizard, several identity synchronization components will be installed on the synchronization computer. These include a new synchronization service, a scheduled task to manage the service, and a new account to run the service for you called AAD_*xxxxxxxxxxxx* where the x characters represent a unique, 12-digit alphanumeric string specific to your organization. You will also have several new Forefront Identity Manager (FIM) security groups added to the local computer, including FIMSyncAdmins (which will contain the account used to install AAD Connect and the AAD_*xxxxxxxxxxxx account)*, *FIMSyncBrowse, FIMSyncJoiners, FIMSyncOperators, and FIMSyncPasswordSet*.

> **TIP** To avoid causing synchronization failures, do not move, remove, or re-permission the AAD_*xxxxxxxxxxxx* account.

To configure synchronization filtering after Azure AD Connect finishes, but before your first synchronization, you will need to use the following steps to only synchronize the Cloud Service OU accounts from the on-premises AD to the Blue Yonder Airlines Azure AD service:

1. On the synchronization computer that you ran the Azure AD Connect Wizard on, launch the Synchronization Service Manager from the Start menu and then select Connectors.

2. With the on-premises AD name highlighted, select Properties from the Action menu.

3. In the connector Properties' dialog box, select the Configure Directory Partitions option in the Connector Designer area and then click Containers to configure connection options.

4. After successfully authenticating using your on-premises credentials, you will see the Select Containers dialog box. From here you can clear all of the represented OUs except for the Cloud Service Users OU, as shown in Figure 4-11.

5. Click OK to close the properties dialog boxes and then use the Run options for the on-premises AD Connector to run the Full Import and Delta Synchronization actions.

> **MORE INFO** You can learn more about synchronization filtering on MSDN at *http://msdn.microsoft.com/en-us/library/azure/dn801051.aspx*.

FIGURE 4-11 The Select Containers dialog box of the Synchronization Service Manager

Force a directory synchronization and verify that it is successful

When you successfully complete the Azure AD Connect Wizard, it will create a scheduled task that will run every three hours to synchronize your on-premises AD with Azure AD. However, if you deselect the option to Synchronize Now on the Azure AD Connect Wizard's summary page, it will disable that scheduled task to give you time to configure synchronization settings, such as the domain partitions (as you have just done).

After customizing your synchronization filtering, and when you are finally ready to synchronize your domain for the first time, you will need to enable the scheduled task so that it will run every three hours thereafter as the AAD_*xxxxxxxxxxxx* account. After you enable the task in Task Scheduler, select Run from the Actions menu (as shown in Figure 4-12) to force an immediate synchronization.

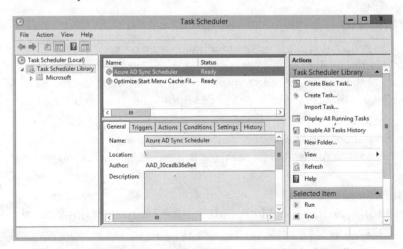

FIGURE 4-12 The Azure AD Sync Scheduler task in the Task Scheduler Library

To verify that the synchronization was successful, simply log on to the Azure Management Portal and review the objects displayed on the Users tab of your Azure AD service instance. If all has gone well, the user account information from the OU that you wanted to synchronize will now be present, similar to what is shown in Figure 4-13.

blue yonder airlines azure ad directory

USERS	GROUPS	APPLICATIONS	DOMAINS	DIRECTORY INTEGRATION	CONFIGURE	REPORTS	LICENSES

DISPLAY NAME	USER NAME	SOURCED FROM
Adina Hagege	Adina@blueyonderairlines.com	Local Active Directory
Alan Steiner	Alan@blueyonderairlines.com	Local Active Directory
Amy Strande	Amy@blueyonderairlines.com	Local Active Directory
Ann Beebe	Ann@blueyonderairlines.com	Local Active Directory
Bruno Torres	Bruno@blueyonderairlines.com	Local Active Directory
David Jaffe	David@blueyonderairlines.com	Local Active Directory
Eric Gilmore	Eva@blueyonderairlines.com	Local Active Directory
Eva Corets	Eric@blueyonderairlines.com	Local Active Directory
Frank Zhang	Frank@blueyonderairlines.com	Local Active Directory
Gabe Frost	Gabe@blueyonderairlines.com	Local Active Directory

FIGURE 4-13 Synchronized user accounts now displayed in The Blue Yonder Airlines Azure AD

Now that you have user objects in Azure AD, you will also need to verify that AD FS is functioning correctly and your users are being authenticated on-premises. You can verify this by simply signing in to the Azure Access Panel at *https://myapps.microsoft.com* using your synchronized organizational credentials. If AD FS is functioning correctly, you will be redirected to your company's default AD FS sign in page as soon as you enter your username and tab into the password box.

Customize branding

Now you have completed configuring directory synchronization from on-premises to Azure AD to enable SSO for Blue Yonder Airlines employees, your next and last task to complete the objectives for this phase of the project will be to provide a consistent look and feel for users signing in across all company websites and services both on the intranet and cloud-based.

Rather than use the basic Microsoft Azure AD Sign-In page used by cloud services shown in Figure 4-3 or the organizational AD FS sign-in page shown in Figure 4-4, you will want to customize each page to add Blue Yonder Airlines branding and provide a familiar and seamless sign-in experience for your users.

Add company branding using the Microsoft Azure Management Portal

You can easily add company branding for Blue Yonder Airlines to the Microsoft Azure AD Sign-In page and the Access Panel from the Azure Management Portal on the Configure tab for the Azure AD directory that you want to customize. Simply select Customize Branding on the Configure tab and then modify the elements that you want to customize. The changes should take affect for all users within about thirty minutes.

> **MORE INFO** The user interface for customizing branding is self-explanatory so it will not be covered in great detail here. You can learn more about the customization options available to you on MSDN at *http://msdn.microsoft.com/library/azure/dn532270.aspx*.

After you customize the sign-in page as shown in Figure 4-14, it now looks more like a standard company website at Blue Yonder Airlines and the Access Panel will also display the company logo rather than the default Microsoft Azure logo.

FIGURE 4-14 Company-branded Azure AD sign-in page

> **TIP** Notice how the sign-in text says to sign in to Windows Azure Active Directory instead of to sign in with your organizational account? This is the Azure AD sign in page that cloud-based users such as those from the default onmicrosoft.com domains will see. This is also the sign-in page shown if you do not configure AD FS for SSO.

Customize the AD FS sign-in page

Because you have configured AD FS and SSO for Blue Yonder Airlines employees, they will not usually be signing in to the default Azure AD sign-in page that was shown in Figure 4-3. Instead of being redirected to a customized Azure AD sign-in page, your users will now be redirected via the Web Application Proxy server computer to the AD FS server's sign-in page for on-premises authentication, so you also need to modify the branding on that page.

It is easy to modify the AD FS sign-in page using Windows PowerShell and the same logo image files you used to customize the Azure AD sign-in page. You can also add company-specific descriptions and links for more information or support.

You can use the following Windows PowerShell commands to customize the on-premises AD FS sign-in page like the Azure AD sign-in page:

- To replace the company name with a company logo file:

```
Set-AdfsWebTheme -TargetName default -Logo @{path="<pathToLogo>.png"}
```

- To replace the default illustration with a custom picture:

```
Set-AdfsWebTheme -TargetName default -Illustration @{path="<pathToLogo>.png"}
```

- To add sign-in page description text:

```
Set-AdfsGlobalWebContent -SignInPageDescriptionText
"<yourHTMLFormattedTextGoesHere>"
```

- To add a helpdesk link:

```
Set-AdfsGlobalWebContent -HelpDeskLink <linkUrl> -HelpDeskLinkText Help
```

- To add a home page link:

```
Set-AdfsGlobalWebContent -HomeLink <linkUrl> -HomeLinkText Home
```

- To add a custom privacy page link:

```
Set-AdfsGlobalWebContent -PrivacyLink <linkUrl> -PrivacyLinkText Privacy
```

If you use all of the these commands, the Windows PowerShell command window will look something like what's shown in Figure 4-15.

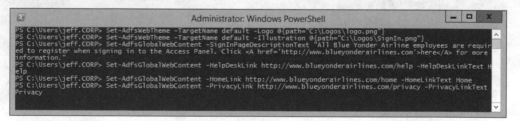

FIGURE 4-15 Windows PowerShell commands to customize the on-premises AD FS sign-in page

> **MORE INFO** You can learn more about the other customizations available to you and image size recommendations on TechNet at *http://technet.microsoft.com/en-us/library/dn280950.aspx*.

After you enter all of the Windows PowerShell commands successfully, you need to verify the changes have taken place by performing an SSO sign-in as a synchronized user. At this point, the AD FS sign-in page should now look something like Figure 4-16 instead of the default image.

FIGURE 4-16 Company-branded on-premises AD FS sign-in page

Congratulations, you have completed the first implementation phase of the EMS project for Blue Yonder Airlines.

## Chapter 5

Device management

Enterprise companies today are more than ever facing the challenges presented by the BYOD trend and searching for ways to support users who bring their own devices to work while at the same time struggling with how to protect company data. To do this, employees must allow company IT departments to manage some aspects of their personal devices to ensure the security of corporate data and compliance with company policies. In general, more and more employees are beginning to use their personal devices to perform some aspects of their daily jobs with the awareness that the company they work for will need to perform certain actions to safeguard company data, including applying security policies, installing software, and performing basic hardware and software inventories of their devices.

As the device management component of EMS, Microsoft Intune is a cloud-based management solution that enables organizations to provide their employees access to business apps and d ata from almost anywhere on almost any device, while also helping to keep company information secure. Using Microsoft Intune you can manage Windows computers and mobile devices including iOS, Android, Windows RT, and Windows Phones. You can deploy policies to help secure corporate data on phones and tablets, perform hardware and software inventories, distribute software, and retire or wipe mobile devices.

Microsoft Intune provides you with a wide range of general PC and device management capabilities as well as functions specific to each. This chapter focuses on preparing you to enroll devices into management with Microsoft Intune and then introduces you to the following device management features of the service: policies, inventory, and selective wipe functionality.

> **TIP** You can learn more about the Mobile Device Management capabilities of Microsoft Intune on TechNet at *http://technet.microsoft.com/en-us/library/dn600287.aspx*.

Preparing for device enrollment

Before you can begin managing devices with Microsoft Intune, you must first configure the service and ensure that you have planned and prepared for the device types that you want to support.

This section describes several key elements of the Microsoft Intune service that you should be familiar with and that you should plan for as you begin preparing to enroll devices into management, including setting the Mobile Device Management (MDM) authority, understanding the device-specific enrollment prerequisites that must be met before your users begin enrolling devices, understanding how to create device enrollment profiles, learning about the Company Portal and how to customize it to create a seamless experience for your users, and finally, understanding how to write and publish custom terms and conditions for use of the service to your users.

Mobile Device Management authority

Before you can enroll mobile devices and begin managing them with Microsoft Intune, you must first prepare the service to accept devices into management. You do this by selecting the check box on the Manage Mobile Devices dialog that is displayed when you select the Mobile Device Management authority setting on the Mobile Device Management page of the Administration workspace in the Microsoft Intune administration console, as shown in Figure 5-1.

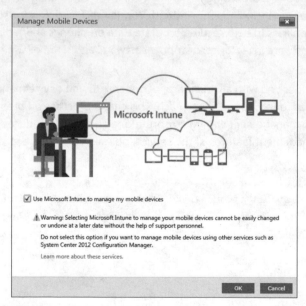

FIGURE 5-1 Setting the Mobile Device Management authority to Microsoft Intune

The Mobile Device Management authority setting determines whether you will manage mobile devices with Microsoft Intune or by using System Center 2012 Configuration Manager with Microsoft Intune integration.

Many organizations already use System Center Configuration Manager 2012 on-premises to manage servers, PCs, and other devices. In this situation, most organizations simply integrate Microsoft Intune with their existing Configuration Manager infrastructure to create a robust hybrid management solution for servers, PCs, and mobile devices when they purchase EMS or standalone Microsoft Intune subscription licenses. While the focus of this book is on using Microsoft Intune standalone, because that technology is included with EMS, you should also know that Microsoft Intune licensing provides non-perpetual use rights for on-premises use of System Center 2012 Configuration Manager and Endpoint Protection (SCEP) to manage as many as five devices per Microsoft Intune-licensed user. This means that you are entitled to install and use System Center 2012 Configuration Manager integrated with Microsoft Intune in a unified device management scenario for the duration of your valid Microsoft Intune subscription. However, if your Microsoft Intune subscription is not renewed in this licensing model, you will need to either stop using the on-premises software or purchase System Center 2012 Configuration Manager licenses.

Real World   Using Configuration Manager for Mobile Device Management

As I talk to customers around the world, I tend to find that mobility fits into existing functional teams inside IT and that often the endpoint management tool of choice for that team is Configuration Manager. As a result, managing mobility and mobile devices often falls to "the Config Man team."

System Center Configuration Manager is unique in that it integrates deeply with Microsoft Intune to enable enterprise mobility. This unique, hybrid architecture gives IT all the benefits of a single pane of glass for device and app management but all the flexibility and ease of deployment that the cloud offers. This hybrid configuration requires that you set Configuration Manager as your MDM authority over Microsoft Intune and from then on you simply manage devices and apps through the System Center Configuration Manager 2012 console.

Setting this up is quite simple. In the Configuration Manager console (2012 SP1 onward), go to the Administration pane and add a Microsoft Intune subscription to your hierarchy. Next, configure your subscription through the Configuration Manager wizard to support specific device types by completing the requirements for those devices. Finally, add the Microsoft Intune site system role and be sure your Active Directory directory synchronization is working.

Simon May (@simonster)
Technical Evangelist for Enterprise Mobility, Microsoft Corporation

Device management prerequisites

Before you can begin managing the different mobile device types supported for management with Microsoft Intune, you will most likely need to perform tasks that meet the operating system-specific requirements for the devices you need to support. For example, to manage iOS devices, you will need an Apple Push Notification service (APNs) certificate; to enroll Windows Phone 8.0 devices, you will need a code-signing certificate from Symantec. Other devices—such as Android devices, Windows RT devices, or Windows 8.1 computers enrolled as devices—have no specific device management prerequisites that must be met before your users can enroll them into management with Microsoft Intune.

There are other code-signing and key requirements that must be met when uploading signed application packages to deploy to devices using Microsoft Intune. This process, called sideloading, enables you to deploy line of business (LOB) apps to devices without having to go through a public application store. However, sideloading applications requires that you have the necessary code-signing certificate as well as sideloading keys obtained from the Microsoft Volume Licensing Service Center (VLSC) previously uploaded into the Microsoft Intune Admin Portal.

> **MORE INFO**   Sideloading apps is beyond the scope of this book, but you can learn more about it on TechNet at *http://technet.microsoft.com/en-us/library/dn646972.aspx*.

The information in this section will help you understand the requirements for iOS and Windows Phone devices as well as how to prepare the Microsoft Intune service to support and manage the mobile device types that your users are bringing to work.

> **TIP**   The actual steps to configure the requirements in this section will be described in further detail in the next chapter.

Prepare to manage iOS devices

Before Microsoft Intune can be used to manage iOS devices, you must first obtain an APNs certificate. This certificate is used to establish an encrypted connection between the APNs and the MDM authority services hosted by Microsoft Intune to enable management of iOS devices.

Before you begin this process, you need an Apple ID associated with an email account from your company. Make sure that you will be able to access this account even if the person originally requesting the APNs certificate leaves the company. You will need that account ID and password not only when you first request the certificate but also when the APNs certificate needs to be renewed.

Configure DNS name resolution for Windows devices

There are several steps that need to be accomplished to manage Windows devices depending on the operating system that you need to support, but one thing these steps all have in common is the need to access an enrollment server during the enrollment process.

When your users try to enroll their devices, they will be prompted for their credentials and their devices must be able to access the enrollment server. Technically, they could manually enter their user names, passwords, and *manage.microsoft.com* to enroll their devices, but that will require all of your users to know the enrollment server name and how to use that name to enroll their devices. A better option is to simply create a CNAME DNS record with your domain registrar for the domain that you registered and that was previously verified in the Microsoft Azure administrator console, for use with your cloud services. Once that is completed, your users will need only their user names and passwords to enroll their Windows devices.

Prepare to manage Windows Phone 8.0 devices

Before you can enroll and manage a Windows Phone 8.0 device, you will need to purchase a code-signing certificate from Symantec using a Windows Phone app developer company publisher ID. You will need that code-signing certificate to sign the Company Portal app (ssp.xap) used by Windows Phone 8.0 devices during device enrollment as well as to sign any LOB apps that you want to deploy to Windows Phone devices.

To prepare for enrolling Windows Phone 8.0 devices, you need to download the Windows Phone 8.0 Company Portal app from the Microsoft download center, install the Windows Phone 8.0 SDK, code-sign the Company Portal app with SignTool.exe included with the SDK, and then upload the signed Company Portal app to the Microsoft Intune Admin Portal before enrolling any Windows Phone 8.0 devices.

Prepare to manage other Windows devices

At this point, you are ready to enroll the remaining supported Windows devices (currently Windows RT, Windows Phone 8.1 devices, and Windows 8.1 computers enrolled as devices) into management with Microsoft Intune without any further configuration required.

Remember that you will not be able to deploy (sideload) LOB applications to any of the Windows devices without first using a Symantec code-signing certificate to sign the application to be deployed and then using the sideloading keys as previously discussed. However, you can still enroll these Windows devices into management and deploy apps from the various app stores to them.

Device enrollment profiles

Device enrollment profiles are used by Microsoft Intune to control how devices are enrolled into the service. Using a device enrollment profile, you can predetermine which device group that devices will become members of and you can set user associations with newly enrolled BYOD devices. At least one device enrollment profile must be specified before devices can be enrolled in Microsoft Intune, so you must plan for, and create, a custom device group to use for the default enrollment profile before users begin enrolling their devices.

The first device enrollment profile you create automatically becomes the default policy applied to BYOD devices. Otherwise, you will need to specify which device enrollment profile to apply to devices enrolling in the service. The default profile will always be assigned to mobile devices enrolled in Microsoft Intune that don't have another profile specified. Figure 5-2 shows an example Device Enrollment Policy configured to assign newly enrolled devices into the custom All BYOD Devices group.

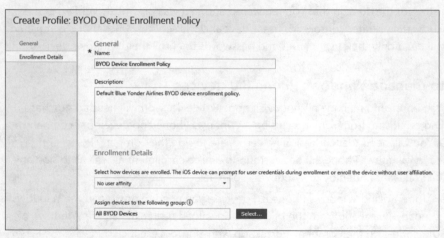

FIGURE 5-2   A default Device Enrollment Policy

The Company Portal

The Company Portal is available both as a website and as a mobile device app that is installed by users on BYOD devices. It enables users to search, browse, and install apps that administrators make available through the Microsoft Intune service; it also enables users to self-manage their devices and profiles. Apps displayed in the Company Portal can be accessed by enrolled devices whether you are connected to the company network or not.

The Company Portal app is available for Windows, Android, or iOS devices in each of the respective company's app stores. Users must download and install the applicable version on their BYOD devices to self-enroll as many as five devices each into the Microsoft Intune management service and gain access to company-managed applications.

Regardless of the device type, or whether the portal is seen on the website or a mobile device app, the Company Portal is composed of three major sections, as shown in Figure 5-3:

- **Apps**   In this section of the Company Portal, users can browse the apps that have been made available to them by their Microsoft Intune administrator. Apps can be sorted by new, by category, or they can simply view all available apps.

- **My Devices**   This section of the Company Portal displays all of the devices that are currently enrolled into the Microsoft Intune service by the logged on user. As a logged on user, you can review the properties of each device, change the display name so that it is easier for you to recognize, perform a factory reset, remove the device from management, or force a policy synchronization to ensure your device has the most recent policy settings applied. You can also perform a remote wipe on certain device types.

- **Contact IT**   In this section of the Company Portal, users can get helpdesk information so that they know whom to contact and how. This information includes not only the tech support person's name but also their phone number, email links, and website information. You can also include additional tech support text to keep users informed of their troubleshooting options.

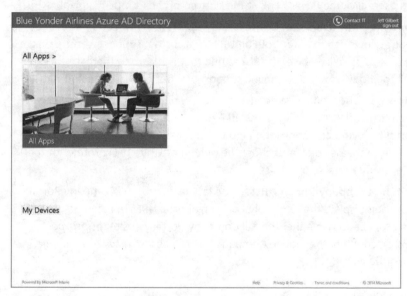

FIGURE 5-3   The Microsoft Intune Company Portal website

Customizing the Company Portal

Just as you need to customize the Azure App Panel to provide a smooth and company-centric experience for your users, you will probably want to do the same with the Company Portal. Many options are available for you to do just that from within the Microsoft Intune Admin Console. The customizations you make here apply equally to both the Company Portal App used by devices and the Company Portal website that is accessed by computers.

While the default Company Portal experience provides basic access to apps, device settings, and IT contact information, it is very basic and without any company branding. To avoid confusing your users and to provide a more seamless and branded experience, you can customize many aspects of the Company Portal, including additional information that will assist your users to get their jobs done and reduce the number of helpdesk calls they might otherwise make.

On the Microsoft Intune Admin Portal page at Admin, Company Portal, you can find the following sections and options for customizing the Company Portal experience for your Microsoft Intune service as described below:

- **Specify Company Name, Company Contact Information And Privacy Statement**.   This section of the Company Portal settings allows you to customize the user experience by displaying the company name (displayed as the title of the Company Portal), IT Department Contact Name, IT Department Phone Number, IT Department Email Address, any additional tech support information you would like displayed (shown when a user clicks the Contact IT option in the top-right corner of the Company Portal), and a company privacy statement URL (this target URL will be opened when users click the Privacy link at the bottom of the Company Portal).

- **Specify A Website That Users Can Contact For Support**.   This section of the customization page allows you to enter both an URL for a custom support website that is hidden from users as well as a website name title that is shown to them. Users can utilize this link to find ways to access online support without calling the helpdesk.

- **Customization**.   This section contains customization options similar to those used to customize the Microsoft Azure Access Panel in Azure AD. Here you can customize the Company Portal with your company logo (and the company name next to the logo if you want it there), a theme color, and either the default or white background for the Windows 8 Company Portal app.

- **Microsoft Intune Company Portal URLs**.   The last section of the Company Portal customization page displays the read-only Company Portal URLs that can be used to review your customizations in either the full Company Portal website (*https://portal. manage.microsoft.com/*) or the mobile Company Portal website (*https://m.manage. microsoft.com/*).

> **TIP**   You can learn more about customizing the Microsoft Intune Company Portal on TechNet at *http://technet.microsoft.com/library/dn646983. aspx#BKMK_ConfigureCompanyPortal*.

Custom company terms and conditions

In addition to providing a link to a custom privacy statement website at the bottom of the Company Portal, you can also publish custom terms and conditions that your users will see when they first log into the Company Portal. You can customize the terms and conditions for accessing the Company Portal on the terms and conditions page of the Microsoft Intune Admin Console at ADMIN, Company Portal, Terms And Conditions.

You can choose whether to force your users to accept the terms and conditions in order to access the Company Portal. If enforced, they will need to accept the terms to gain access regardless of whether the device they are using is already enrolled in management, but they will need to accept the terms and conditions only once regardless of how many devices they have enrolled into the Microsoft Intune service. If you require users to accept company terms and conditions, but they do not accept them, they will be denied access to the Company Portal and the apps and capabilities available there. They will also need to unenroll all of their devices in management, as shown in Figure 5-4.

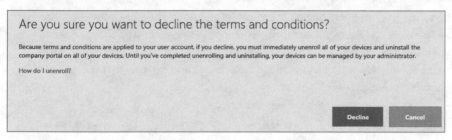

FIGURE 5-4   The decline terms and conditions confirmation dialog box

You can easily update the terms and conditions to make a new version available at any time from within the Microsoft Intune Admin Console and require that users agree to the updated terms and conditions in order to continue accessing the Company Portal.

By using the built-in Terms and Conditions Report made available in the Reports workspace of the Admin Console, it is very easy to see which users have agreed to the terms and conditions, which version they agreed to, and when they agreed to them. If you need to keep a record of this information, you can also easily export it as either a .csv or .html file.

Deploying policies

Microsoft Intune policies are really just groups of settings that control features on computers and mobile devices. These policies are easy to create and based on templates of either recommended or custom settings that enable you to configure common mobile device settings on Android, iOS, and Windows devices as well as configure software and computer management (including firewall settings) on PCs. You can also configure Conditional Access policies that block access to Microsoft Exchange email if the device in use is not enrolled into Microsoft Intune or not in compliance with other compliance policies that you set. You configure and deploy Microsoft Intune policies from within the Policy workspace in the Admin Console, as shown in Figure 5-5.

FIGURE 5-5 The Policy workspace of the Admin Console

It is a good idea to create and deploy Microsoft Intune policies before your users begin enrolling their devices to ensure the process is as smooth as possible and they are not surprised when settings change after they enroll their devices into management. Read the following policy sections carefully and plan for the settings and policies that you will need to implement before you begin enrolling devices.

> **TIP**   When you create a policy that uses the recommended settings, the name of the new policy is a combination of the template name, date, and time. When you edit the policy, the name updates with the time and date of the edit.

Configuration policies

Just as the name implies, Microsoft Intune configuration policies are used to manage expected configuration settings on computers and devices enrolled into the service. This section describes at a high level some of the available configuration policy capabilities of Microsoft Intune as an introduction to get you started planning for your deployment, but does not attempt to describe every policy template or setting in great detail.

> **MORE INFO**   You can learn more about the configuration policies available for Microsoft Intune, including software policy configurations, on TechNet at *http://technet.microsoft. com/en-us/library/dn743712.aspx*.

Common mobile device settings

This section of the Policy workspace in the Microsoft Intune Admin Console is where you configure the default Mobile Device Security Policy. This policy template contains Mobile Device Security Policy settings that are used to configure password settings and encryption requirements.

It's probably a good idea to begin with this policy template as you start to plan how you will manage mobile devices in your enterprise. It covers most of the basic configuration requirements that enterprises want and need and it will apply to all mobile device types without the need to make separate configuration policies for each device type.

When you create and deploy a default Mobile Device Security Policy to your users, the following settings are enabled and applied by default:

- A password is required to unlock the mobile device. It can be either numeric or alpha-numeric. If alphanumeric, it must include a minimum of one character set used (from the four available: uppercase, lowercase, symbols, or numbers).

- The minimum password length is four characters.

- Simple passwords are not allowed (for example, passwords such as 1234 or 1111).

- The number of times an incorrect password can be entered before the device is automatically wiped is set to four.

- The time, in minutes, of inactivity that will be allowed before the screen turns off is set to 15.

- Encryption is enforced on mobile devices.

- Devices that do not fully support the configured settings can still access Exchange ActiveSync. This should not be a problem with the default mobile device settings, but if you configure additional settings beyond the default settings, this setting might be necessary.

These are certainly not the only settings available to be configured in the default Mobile Device Security Policy, but they are the only ones that are enabled by default. These should be used as a baseline as you begin planning what policy settings you will need to configure to fully support the device types your users are bringing to work and what additional, device-specific configuration policies you will need to implement to meet your organizational goals and company security policy requirements.

> **MORE INFO**   You can read more about the available security policy settings on TechNet at *http://technet.microsoft.com/en-us/library/dn646984.aspx.*

Android devices

The configuration policies available for you to set for Android devices include the ability to specify apps that users should, or should not, use while enrolled in your Microsoft Intune service. To check compliance with this policy, you can view reports to see when noncompliant apps are installed or used. You can also configure kiosk mode for Android devices to lock them down and allow only certain features or applications to work.

Various profile options are also available to be configured for Android devices that make connecting to Exchange ActiveSync email (for Samsung KNOX 4.0 and later devices) possible without user interaction and enabling access to corporate resources via configurable trusted certificate, SCEP, VPN, and Wi-Fi profile policy options.

iOS devices

Just like with Android device policies, you can set iOS-specific policies to identify specific apps that users should, or should not, use while enrolled in Microsoft Intune. Again, you can use reports to view compliance with this policy setting and you can configure kiosk mode for iOS devices.

Similar to the available Android settings, you can use iOS configuration policies to configure email profiles for Exchange ActiveSync settings and you can configure network access with trusted certificate and SCEP profiles as well as configure VPN and Wi-Fi profile settings centrally without the need for users to configure these settings themselves.

iOS device configuration policies also include an option to deploy configuration profiles that you create using the Apple Configurator tool. This capability is useful when you want to set a configuration setting for iOS that is not included in the default options for configuration policy settings within Microsoft Intune. You can use the Apple Configurator to easily capture settings that you can then deploy to iPhone, iPad, and iPod touch devices.

> **MORE INFO**   You can learn more about the Apple Configurator and download it from the Mac App Store at *https://itunes.apple.com/us/app/apple-configurator/id434433123?mt=12.*

Windows devices

Again, very similar to Android and iOS policies, you can specify apps that users should, and should not use, but with Windows Phone devices (Windows phone 8.1 and later), rather than just reporting noncompliant apps from being installed or used, you can block the usage of those noncompliant apps.

The same email, trusted certificate, SCEP, and VPN profile configurations are available for Windows devices as for Android and iOS devices when creating a Windows device configuration policy.

Additionally, with Windows devices, you can create Windows Phone OMA-URI[1] (Open Mobile Alliance Uniform Resource Identifier) policies to control functionality of Windows Phone devices. By using OMA-URI settings, you can set Windows Phone settings that are unavailable in the default configuration settings similar to the way you can use the Apple Configurator to set configuration settings on iOS for settings unavailable in the default configuration setting options for that device type.

Computers

In addition to mobile devices, traditional computers can also be managed by installing the Microsoft Intune computer client agent on them. The configuration policy settings available for computers include settings for software updates, Endpoint Protection, Windows Firewall, and other information displayed to users on the Microsoft Intune Center that is installed with the Microsoft Intune client agent, as shown in Figure 5-6.

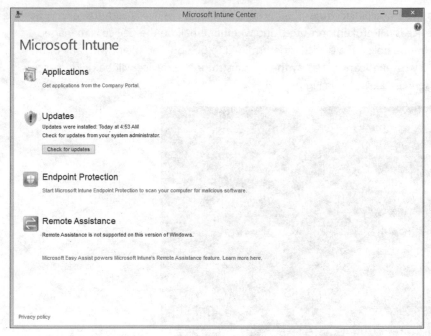

FIGURE 5-6 The Microsoft Intune Center

The Microsoft Intune Center runs in the system tray and allows users to request remote assistance, run anti-malware scans, and manage software updates for their computers. The configuration policy settings for the Microsoft Intune Center also include options for providing tech support or helpdesk information to users on managed computers similar to the support information displayed on the Company Portal.

---

[1] You can learn more about OMA-URI settings for Windows Phones on TechNet at *http://technet.microsoft. com/en-us/library/dn499787.aspx*.

Other Microsoft Intune computer agent settings are used to configure Endpoint Protection scans to help protect computers from malware infections, to exclude folders from virus scans, and to set the frequency for updating both Endpoint Protection and Windows updates.

The final computer configuration policy template setting is used to manage Windows Firewall settings on Microsoft Intune computer clients. The settings available in this template allow you to turn on Windows Firewall, block incoming connections, manage user notifications, and configure exceptions for specific network profiles.

Compliance policies

Compliance policies are used to enforce company compliance requirements when managing devices with Microsoft Intune. While configuration policies are used to configure features and device settings, compliance policies are meant to enforce certain settings to either allow or deny access to the Microsoft Intune service and company resources.

You can configure compliance rules that include advanced password settings, encryption, whether the device is jail-broken or rooted, and whether email on the device is managed by a Microsoft Intune policy. If a device is determined to be non-compliant with any of the compliance policy settings configured by the administrator, the device will be denied access to company resources, as shown in Figure 5-7.

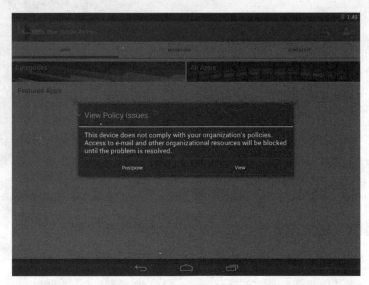

FIGURE 5-7   The View Policy Issues dialog box displayed when a device is noncompliant with company policy

Conditional access policies

Conditional access policies are used by Microsoft Intune to restrict access to Exchange email and ensure that corporate email and documents are synchronized only on phones and tablets that are managed by your company. They are configured and defined by rules, such as which user groups will be targeted to block email based on noncompliance with Microsoft Intune policies and how devices that cannot enroll with Microsoft Intune will or will not be allowed to access Exchange email. If a compliance policy is not deployed, the Conditional Access Policy will treat the device as compliant and allow access to Exchange email. Using conditional access policies, you can restrict access to either Exchange on-premises or Exchange Online (O365).

To use conditional access policies with Exchange on-premises, you must first deploy the on-premises Exchange connector that connects Microsoft Intune service to Microsoft Exchange on-premises to allow you to manage devices through the Microsoft Intune console. Then, to control access to Exchange on-premises for devices not managed by Microsoft Intune, enable the rules that block access by the users in the Microsoft Intune user groups that are specified in the Conditional Access Policy.

Exchange Online conditional access policies are used to block email apps from accessing Exchange Online when devices are either noncompliant with Microsoft Intune compliance policies or not managed by Microsoft Intune and belong to users who are in the Active Directory security groups targeted by the policy.

However, before you can configure the conditional access policies for Exchange Online, you must first configure the Microsoft Intune service-to-service connector. To configure this connector, you must be signed in to the Microsoft Intune Admin Console with an account that has Exchange Online administrative rights. The email address of the currently logged-on user will be used to complete the hosted connection between Microsoft Intune and Exchange Online.

Once the connection is established to either Exchange on-premises or Exchange Online, Microsoft Intune will synchronize new mobile devices and device management status and display those in the Groups workspace in the Microsoft Intune Admin Console. The management status is displayed in the Management Channel column and will define one of the following for each device accessing Exchange email:

- **Managed By Exchange ActiveSync** These devices are accessing Exchange email but they are not managed by Microsoft Intune.

- **Managed By Microsoft Intune** These devices are managed by Microsoft Intune but they are not accessing Exchange email.

- **Managed By Microsoft Intune And Exchange ActiveSync** These devices are both managed by Microsoft Intune and accessing Exchange email.

When a device is a member of a group to which a Conditional Access Policy is targeted, devices that display Managed By Exchange ActiveSync will be blocked unless they are in a group that has been marked exempt from the policy. To avoid blocking Exchange email access without notifying them first, you can run a mobile device inventory report to find email addresses for users with devices that are managed by Exchange ActiveSync who will soon be blocked so that you can notify them before enabling the Conditional Access Policy.

After you enable a Conditional Access Policy, you can easily see which devices have been blocked from accessing Exchange email from the Microsoft Intune dashboard. There, the Blocked Devices From Exchange tile shows the number of blocked devices and links to more information.

Exchange ActiveSync policies

The settings configured in this page of the Policy workspace are applied to mobile devices that are connected to Exchange with a service connector in place whether or not they are managed by Microsoft Intune. Here you can add platform exception rules based on mobile device families and models and configure a default rule for devices not covered by a platform exception rule.

When users are blocked from accessing Exchange due to a Conditional Access Policy, they will receive an email that provides instructions about how to enroll their devices. You can customize that email by defining a custom user notification message using HTML text that will be included in an email sent to users whose access to email has been blocked, as shown in Figure 5-8.

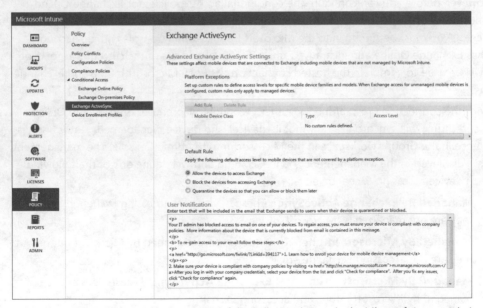

FIGURE 5-8 The Exchange ActiveSync page of the Policy workspace in the Microsoft Intune Admin Console

Policy conflicts

With so many policies being applied to user groups, it is almost inevitable that policies will eventually conflict. When that happens, the depth of the group in the Microsoft Intune group structure helps determine which policy will take precedence.

When policy settings have been configured for groups that conflict, and a user is in both groups, the policy applied to the group that is the deepest in the group structure as defined in the Groups workspace in the Microsoft Intune Admin Console wins and is applied. However, if two or more conflicting policies are applied to the same group, the policy that was updated last (and thus has the most recent Last Modified Time) will apply.

Managing inventory

Microsoft Intune collects information about both computers and mobile devices in use in your organization. You can use this data to discover hardware information about the devices you manage as well as the software that is being run on them.

You can also use the inventory information collected about computers and mobile devices in use for your organization to understand the hardware needs of your users and to plan for future hardware upgrades and replacement device purchases. Additional detected software reports can help you to better understand what software is installed on computers in your organization, including the software versions.

Computer inventory

Computer hardware inventory information is available for viewing by running the Computer Inventory Reports from the Reports workspace in the Microsoft Intune Admin Console. In addition to the name, make, and model of client computers, you can also review the following information about client computers in use in your environment from this report:

- Chassis type
- Operating system
- TPM version
- Disk space information (total, used, free, and OS disk name)
- Physical memory installed
- Processor information (name, architecture, and CPU speed)
- IP address
- Serial number
- Last user to log on
- Last updated time stamp

Mobile device inventory

The mobile device inventory report is used to review mobile device inventory information. Similar to the computer inventory report, the mobile device inventory report contains much more than just the name, make, and model of mobile devices enrolled in the Microsoft Intune service, including:

- Device operating system and version
- Manufacturer
- Management channel
- If the device is registered in Azure AD
- If the device is compliant or not
- Email address for the user who enrolled the device
- Exchange ActiveSync ID
- If the device is jail-broken or rooted
- Unique Device ID
- Serial number
- Storage space (total and free)
- The last four digits of the telephone number for the device (if applicable)
- IMEI (International Mobile Station Equipment Identity)
- MEID (Mobile Equipment Identifier)
- Wi-Fi MAC address
- Subscriber (mobile phone carrier name)
- Cellular technology (CDMA, GSM, and so on)
- When the device was enrolled
- When the inventory was last updated

Performing full and selective wipes

Microsoft Intune provides several capabilities to help protect your company data from falling into the wrong hands. If a device is lost or stolen, Microsoft Intune administrators can perform several remote actions on the device, including changing a compromised passcode or issuing a remote lock command.

However, by far the most powerful data protection feature that Microsoft Intune makes available to you and your users is the ability to remotely wipe a mobile device to remove company data or even just factory-reset the device. This feature can be very useful when you need to retire a device from use, either when you need to replace it or when a person leaves the company. If a device is lost or stolen, you will also want to be sure to get all company information off of the device as soon as possible and the data-wipe commands usually take only about 15 minutes or so to reach the device. Administrators can perform remote wipe functions from the Microsoft Intune Admin Console and users can perform wipes on their enrolled devices from the Company Portal to reset them to factory condition.

Selective device wipes

By compartmentalizing company data and personal data, Microsoft Intune is capable of selectively wiping only company data on users' devices while leaving all of their personal information intact and untouched. This can be useful when a person leaves the company and the device is retired from management or when a user simply wants to replace his personal device and give that device to a friend or relative.

Microsoft Intune administrators can perform a selective wipe on a device simply by right-clicking a device name in the Admin Console and selecting the Retire/Wipe action. At that point, a dialog box similar to the one shown in Figure 5-9 is displayed, confirming the decision to wipe the device.

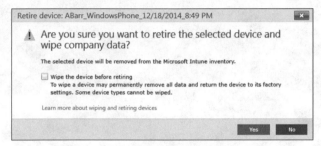

FIGURE 5-9   The Retire Device confirmation dialog box

If there is a need to perform a full device wipe, then select the Wipe The Device Before Retiring check box before continuing. Otherwise, click Yes; a selective wipe of company data will occur, removing all company data from the device.

Full device wipes

If a user's device is lost or stolen, there is no need to contact the helpdesk or wait until the weekend is over to deal with the issue. Users can simply log onto the Company Portal and perform a reset on their enrolled personal devices, as shown in Figure 5-10. This action will perform a full data wipe to restore the device to its factory settings without the user even having to know where the device is.

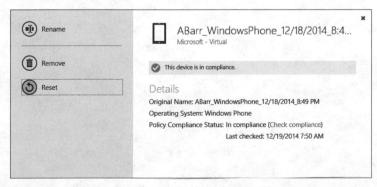

FIGURE 5-10   The factory reset option for devices in the Company Portal

## Chapter 6

Implementing device management

Chapter 5 covered how device management can be used to help meet the challenges brought about by implementing BYOD in enterprise environments to support both company-owned and employee-owned devices. The chapter also described the business requirements to keep company data secure, mobile device usage policies that need to be enforced, and how employees must accept these requirements as a compromise to enabling the flexibility for them to get their jobs done on almost any device and from almost anywhere.

In this chapter, you again adopt the persona of the senior enterprise administrator for Blue Yonder Airlines and work to address the requirements of the second phase of the EMS implementation plan described at the end of Chapter 2. Remember that in this phase, you are responsible for preparing for, and successfully implementing, device management for the company, and the airline's employees, to fully support BYOD.

Scenario description

As the senior enterprise administrator for Blue Yonder Airlines, you are responsible for planning, designing, and implementing the company's EMS solution. You have completed the first phase of the EMS implementation plan to configure hybrid identity leveraging the existing on-premises Active Directory with Azure Active Directory (Azure AD) to populate cloud service users successfully. Now you must address the device management requirements to support company-owned devices as well as all of the personal devices being brought to work by Blue Yonder Airlines employees without your knowledge.

You know that Blue Yonder Airlines has made investments in iPads that are used by many of the pilots and stewards employed by the company at remote locations and the Windows Phones used by the IT department, but you are also aware of the fact that several employees are using their personal iPhones and Android devices to access corporate email and resources. Company employees accessing corporate data through unmanaged devices represents a security risk that must be mitigated during this phase of the implementation plan. Therefore, you need to plan to support all devices in use as well as implement policies to keep corporate data secure regardless of what device is being used.

Implementation goals

Building on the capabilities enabled by hybrid identity, you now need to address the following implementation goals to successfully complete the second phase of the EMS rollout for Blue Yonder Airlines:

- Prepare the Microsoft Intune service for device enrollment as described in Chapter 5.
- Address the Mobile Device Management (MDM) enrollment considerations for iOS and Windows devices.
- Successfully enroll employee devices into the Microsoft Intune service instance managed by Blue Yonder Airlines IT.
- Restrict access to corporate email to only those devices managed by Microsoft Intune and in compliance with Blue Yonder Airlines company policies.

Solution diagram

To meet the EMS implementation goals for the second phase of the EMS project, you will need to implement the solution shown in Figure 6-1.

> **TIP** This solution diagram is meant to provide a high-level overview and basic description of the intended solution architecture. Planning and design considerations for each element of the solution will be further described in the next section.

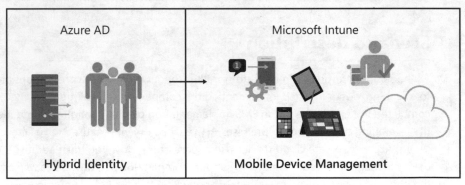

FIGURE 6-1 Building on hybrid identity to implement MDM to manage devices and control access to corporate email

This solution is comprised of the following two pieces:

- **Hybrid identity** The hybrid identity capabilities that were enabled earlier in the EMS implementation will be leveraged to ensure that only authorized and authenticated Blue Yonder Airlines employees will be able to enroll their devices into management or access the Company Portal.

- **Mobile Device Management**   Once properly authenticated, Blue Yonder Airlines employees will be able to enroll their mobile devices into management by Microsoft Intune. Their devices must be managed, and in compliance with company policy, before they will be able to access corporate email via Exchange Online.

Planning and designing the solution

Now that you have developed your implementation goals and the proposed solution, you need to be sure that you understand all of the planning and design considerations that must be addressed for this phase to be completed successfully.

Although many of these considerations were introduced at a high-level in Chapter 5, you should carefully review the information in this section to be sure you are ready to put your plan into action to implement MDM in support of Blue Yonder Airlines' BYOD policy.

> **TIP**   This planning and design section is meant to provide you with additional details about the components and considerations to consider while implementing MDM with Microsoft Intune. The next section will guide you through the actual implementation steps and explain each component.

Microsoft Intune service configuration considerations

As you learned in Chapter 5, Microsoft Intune is the device management component of EMS that enables organizations to provide their employees access to apps and data from almost anywhere on almost any device while also helping to keep company information secure. As you prepare to implement MDM for Blue Yonder Airlines, you need to consider how you will customize your Microsoft Intune service instance to best support the customized and specific needs of Blue Yonder Airlines.

Mobile Device Management authority

The very first thing you need to do to support device management with Microsoft Intune is to set the MDM authority. This step prepares the Microsoft Intune service to accept enrollment requests and configures it as a standalone management service rather than one integrated with a System Center Configuration Manager 2012 R2 hierarchy.

As you plan for this step, carefully consider whether you will take advantage of the System Center Configuration Manager 2012 R2 license usage rights that come with EMS. If you set the MDM authority to use Microsoft Intune to manage your mobile devices and later decide to configure a hybrid management environment, you will not be able to easily modify the MDM authority setting to enable that alternate scenario.

Device enrollment profiles

Microsoft Intune uses device enrollment profiles to control which device group a newly enrolled device is automatically added to. As you plan for enabling users to enroll their devices from the Company Portal, you need to create at least one device enrollment profile.

When creating the device enrollment profile, consider what to name the profile and the description you will give it to ensure other administrators know why you have created the profile. Other details for device enrollment to plan for include whether you will prompt iOS users during enrollment to support user affiliation and the device group you will use to support service enrollment for devices associated with this profile. You will need to either create a custom device group or select an existing custom device group from the Groups workspace of the Microsoft Intune Admin Console that will be referenced by the enrollment profile. If you create multiple device enrollment profiles, be sure to set the one that you want to use as the default enrollment profile.

Customize the Company Portal

The Blue Yonder Airlines Company Portal is the way that most, if not all, BYOD devices will be enrolled into management and it is also where your users will go to access apps, maintain their profile information, and look for helpdesk contact information.

As the enterprise administrator, you should plan to present a professional and familiar experience to your users. Customizing the Company Portal to provide a company-branded experience will give your users confidence that they are enabling MDM for a trusted entity. In addition to displaying the company name as the title of the Company Portal, be sure that you are ready to customize the Company Portal with the following:

- **Company contact information**   This information is used by Blue Yonder Airlines employees to determine how to contact the IT department. Here you need to provide the IT department contact name, phone number, email address, and any additional information you want displayed to end users on the Company Portal.

  This is also where you can provide a link to the Blue Yonder Airlines privacy statement webpage that discloses some or all of the ways that the company will use, disclose, or manage collected employee data. Users can access the target URL by clicking the privacy link at the bottom of the Company Portal.

- **Support contact information**   You can provide the address to the support website to which you want to send end users who have questions. To complete this information, you need to know the support website URL and you should consider using a friendly name for the link that will be displayed on the Company Portal. If you do not enter a support website URL or friendly name, then Go To IT Website is displayed on the Contact IT page in the Company Portal.

- **Company branding**   The final Company Portal customization to consider is how you will brand it to provide Blue Yonder Employees a familiar experience. Consider what theme color you will choose from the following available colors: blue, red, orange, green, or purple.

You also need to upload two versions of the company logo; one to be displayed when the Company Portal background is white and another to show when the selected Company Portal theme color is in use. In either case, the logo file itself must be no larger than 400 x 100 pixels and 750 KB.

Terms and conditions

This part of implementation planning focuses on defining custom terms and conditions that all Blue Yonder Airlines employees need to aware of, and agree to, before accessing the Company Portal and using their personal devices at work. You will probably need to work with the Legal department and HR department to define the final text to display when users log on to the Company Portal for the first time.

In addition to the content, you need to carefully consider whether to enforce acceptance of the terms and conditions before allowing users to access company resources and enroll their devices into management. If you require acceptance of the terms and conditions, as shown in Figure 6-2, each Blue Yonder Airlines employee logging on to the Company Portal must accept those terms to continue. If an employee does not accept the terms and conditions, he will be denied access to the Company Portal. However, if the employee who doesn't accept the terms and conditions already has a device under management, it will remain so until he uninstalls the Company Portal from his device.

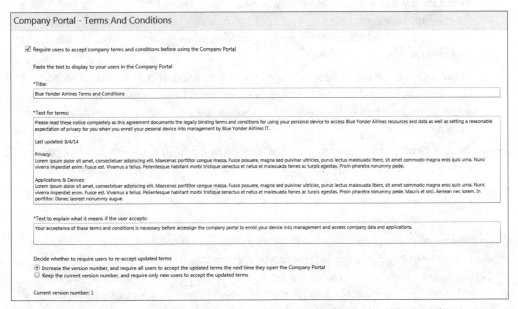

FIGURE 6-2 Example terms and conditions as defined in the Microsoft Intune Admin Console

Policies

Before you or your users begin enrolling devices, you need to carefully plan for and deploy both configuration and compliance policies that will take effect as soon as a Blue Yonder Airlines employee's device is enrolled into management. It is a good idea to plan carefully and document completely each of the policy settings that you will put into effect to ensure that you are meeting your implementation goals and ensuring compliance with company mobile device configuration policies.

Configuration policies

Configuration policies make it easy for your users to use their personal devices at work and ensure that the devices being used are properly configured in accordance with company policies.

The first configuration policy that you should plan for is the basic Mobile Device Security Policy. This policy is used to ensure that all mobile devices are configured for basic security settings immediately after they are enrolled into management. For this configuration policy, you need to determine what template settings need to be enforced according to company policy. In addition to common security requirements, such as requiring a password, you also need to consider the following settings:

- **Cloud Policy Settings**   Be sure that you plan whether to allow end-user devices to access cloud resources, such as iCloud, Work Folders, or Google backups.

- **Email Policy Settings**   These policy settings control how email accounts and related functionality are configured on your user's mobile devices. You can control whether users can download email attachments, how long email is synchronized on the devices, and several other email-related settings.

- **Application Settings**   These settings control how users and mobile devices interact with applications while under management. You can pre-configure several browser settings, define whether the device app store will be available, and even allow or deny gaming options.

- **Device Capability Settings**   The final section of the Mobile Device Security Policy is very powerful and will enable you to configure the physical devices used by Blue Yonder Airlines at a very granular level. These settings allow you to control hardware capabilities, such as the camera, Wi-Fi, Bluetooth, and other aspects of device usage (such as data roaming and copy and paste functionality).

In addition to the basic mobile device security settings that will be applied to all mobile devices that are enrolled into management, you can simplify user access to company data and email by pre-defining wireless connections, VPN connections, and email settings. This will enable them to automatically join local Wi-Fi networks and access corporate network resources or email effortlessly and without any manual configurations on their part. While Wi-Fi and VPN profiles are not within the scope of your initial deployment, you will want to deploy and manage email profiles for your users.

Pre-configuring these email profile settings will make it much easier for your users and will save both you and your users a lot of time and increase productivity. To configure these settings for Android (Samsung KNOX 4.0 and later), iOS (5 and later), and Windows Phones (8 and later), you should have the following information ready:

- Exchange ActiveSync host name
- Account name you will display on the device
- Username (either the User Principle Name or Primary SMTP Address)
- Email address (either the User Principle Name or Primary SMTP Address)
- Authentication method you will use

In addition, you should also plan for how you will configure several other synchronization options:

- Number of days of email to synchronize (from three days to unlimited)
- Sync schedule (from manual to as messages arrive)
- Whether or not to use SSL
- Determine the content types to synchronize (Email, Contacts, Calendar, and Tasks)

> **TIP** There are many more options and configuration policy settings that go beyond the scope of this book that you should review and consider implementing as part of your configuration policy settings. You can learn more about the Mobile Device Security Policy settings on TechNet at *http://technet.microsoft.com/en-us/library/dn646984.aspx* and other general configuration policy settings at *http://technet.microsoft.com/en-us/library/dn743712.aspx*.

Compliance policies

After you have completed your research and fully documented the configuration policy settings that you will deploy to users who are accessing company resources from mobile devices, you must consider how you will enforce compliance to those settings.

While configuration policies will set the various aspects about how mobile devices are used in the Blue Yonder Airlines enterprise environment, you know that several users will either accidentally or purposely not comply with those recommended settings. To ensure that your users are in compliance with the configuration you have defined, you will need to define and deploy a compliance policy that will enforce compliance on password settings, encryption, whether a device is jailbroken, and whether email accounts for iOS (6+) devices must be managed by Microsoft Intune.

Enrolled devices will synchronize with the Microsoft Intune service on a regular basis to check for updated policy settings and at the same time they will also evaluate policy compliance. If the device is found to be noncompliant, messages are displayed to users on their devices, giving them about an hour to bring their devices into compliance, as shown in Figure 6-3. As you plan for the compliance settings that you will enforce, you should also consider the impact of these messages on end users who have previously been using unmanaged devices and are not accustomed to these kinds of messages and restrictions being placed on them. This might be a good scenario to cover on your tech support website.

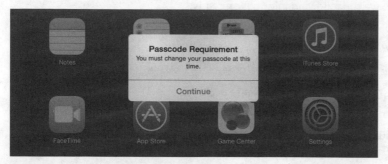

FIGURE 6-3 A user is informed of noncompliance with company policy

Conditional access policies

The final policy that you need to plan for before implementing MDM for Blue Yonder Airlines is the Conditional Access Policy. This policy helps you to meet the implementation goal of restricting access to corporate email to only those devices managed by Microsoft Intune. Because Blue Yonder Airlines uses Office 365, you will need to configure the Conditional Access For Exchange Online Policy.

Before you can create the Conditional Access Policy, you first need to set up the service-to-service connector to link your Microsoft Intune service with your Exchange online environment. Once that is set up and working, you need to plan for creating the Exchange Online policy itself.

As you plan for the settings for this policy that will block access to email if a device is noncompliant, another prerequisite is to create or identify an Active Directory security group already synchronized with Azure AD that you will apply the policy to. If you want to exempt some users from this policy, you can also identify a security group to be exempted as part of the policy. The final planning step for this policy is to determine whether you will allow or block access to email from devices that are not supported by Microsoft Intune.

Mobile Device Management enrollment considerations

With the Microsoft Intune service implementation steps properly planned for, you can turn your attention to preparing for enrolling the different types of mobile devices that you will need to support as part of the Enterprise Mobility Strategy for Blue Yonder Airlines.

You know that users are already bringing their Android, iOS, and Windows Phone devices to work, so you will plan for all possible devices. As you learned in Chapter 5, Android devices do not have any device-specific requirements that you need to plan for as you prepare for device enrollment. However, you will need to plan for and configure several external dependencies to support iOS and Windows devices to be successfully enrolled into Microsoft Intune.

iOS devices

To enable iOS device enrollment, you need to obtain an Apple Push Notification service (APNs) certificate. To get this certificate, download an APNs certificate request from within the Microsoft Intune Admin Console and then upload it, using an Apple ID, to the Apple Push Certificates Portal. After you successfully obtain the APNs certificate, usually named something like *MDM_Microsoft Corporation_Certificate.pem*, you save it locally so that you can upload it into the Microsoft Intune Admin Console as part of the implementation process.

Remember that this certificate will need to be periodically renewed, so ensure that you will have access to the Apple ID and password used to request the APNs certificate even if the person who originally requests it leaves the company. You can easily create an Apple ID for this purpose at *https://appleid.apple.com/account*.

To obtain the Blue Yonder Airlines APNs certificate, you must plan for and complete the following actions:

1. **Generate an APN certificate signing request file**   This request file (.csr) is created from within the Microsoft Intune Admin Console by navigating to Administration, Mobile Device Management, iOS, Upload An APNs Certificate and then clicking the option to Download The APNs Certificate Request. Give the certificate request file a name and then save it locally.

2. **Sign in to the Apple Push Certificates Portal**   Use your company Apple ID credentials to sign in to the Apple Push Certificates Portal at *http://go.microsoft.com/fwlink/?LinkId=261984*.

3. **Create the APNs certificate**   Select the Create A Certificate option to begin the process of creating the APNs certificate. Next, read and accept the terms of use to continue.

4. **Upload the APNs certificate request (.csr) file**   On this page, you can enter notes as a description for the push certificate or just click Browse to select the .csr file that you created in Step 1 that will be used to create the certificate when you select the Upload option.

5. **Download the certificate**   The completed APNs certificate should now be created and displayed in the available certificates listed for the Apple ID that you have used, as shown in Figure 6-4. Click the Download button to download the .pem file locally.

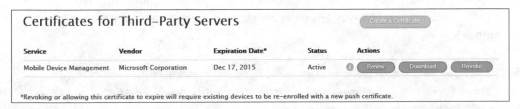

FIGURE 6-4 The APNs certificate as shown in the Apple Push Certificates Portal

Windows Phone 8.0

To prepare for enrolling Windows Phone 8.0 devices, download the Windows Phone 8.0 Company Portal app from the Microsoft Download Center, install the Windows Phone 8.0 Software Development Kit (SDK), code-sign the Company Portal app with SignTool.exe included with the SDK, and then upload the signed Company Portal app to the Microsoft Intune Admin Console before enrolling any Windows Phone 8.0 devices.

Follow theses steps to code-sign the Windows Phone 8.0 Company Portal app in preparation for enrolling those devices:

1. Register as an app developer and get a company publisher ID at the Windows Phone Dev Center at *http://dev.windows.com/join*.

2. Use the company publisher ID to purchase an enterprise mobile code-signing certificate from Symantec at *https://products.websecurity.symantec.com/orders/enrollment/microsoftCert.do*.

3. Download the Windows Phone 8 Company Portal app from the Microsoft Download Center at *http://www.microsoft.com/download/details.aspx?id=36060*.

4. Download and install the Windows Phone 8.0 SDK at *http://www.microsoft.com/download/details.aspx?id=35471*.

5. Use SignTool.exe[1], installed with the Windows Phone 8 SDK, to sign the Windows Phone 8.0 Company Portal app with the Symantec code-signing certificate.

> **TIP** You will need to upload both the APNs certificate and the signed Windows Phone 8.0 Company Portal app later during the implementation phase.

Windows device name resolution

The final step that you must plan for in preparation for enrolling mobile devices is name resolution for Windows devices. To complete this step, you need to create a DNS CNAME record with your domain registrar to enable Windows devices to locate the enrollment server.

Specifically, you create a CNAME record that redirects name resolution requests for enterpriseenrollment.<*yourdomainnamegoeshere*> to manage.microsoft.com. For example, if the publicly registered, and Azure-verified, domain name that you want to use is blueyonderairlines.com, your DNS CNAME record would need to redirect DNS requests for enterpriseenrollment.blueyonderairlines.com to manage.microsoft.com, as shown in Figure 6-5.

> **TIP** If you do not have access or permissions to modify your public domain DNS records, you will need to plan for how you will accomplish this DNS zone file update before you begin enrolling Windows devices.

---

[1] You can learn more about SignTool.exe at *http://msdn.microsoft.com/en-us/library/8s9b9yaz(v=vs.110).aspx*.

FIGURE 6-5 An example DNS CNAME record to enable enrollment server name resolution for Windows devices

Implementing device management

Now that you have a deeper understanding of the components involved and you have completed the prerequisite planning to successfully implement MDM for Blue Yonder Airlines, you are ready to take action to complete phase 2 of the EMS implementation plan. You will start by preparing the Microsoft Intune service for device enrollment, then enroll devices, and, finally, ensure that access to corporate email is safeguarded using conditional access.

Prepare the Microsoft Intune service for device enrollment

Follow the steps in this section to configure Blue Yonder Airlines' Microsoft Intune service for mobile device enrollment and management. Using the information gained during your implementation planning, you are now ready to properly configure the service so that your users can seamlessly enroll their devices into management, that those mobile devices are kept in compliance with all company policies, and that users can easily access corporate data, apps, and email.

Set the Mobile Device Management authority

The first step to be taken in the Microsoft Intune Admin Console to begin the process of managing mobile devices with the service is to set the MDM authority to Microsoft Intune. Doing this also enables other MDM settings and options that will be configured later.

Complete the following steps to set the MDM authority to Microsoft Intune:

1. Sign in to the Microsoft Intune Admin Console with administrator permissions.

2. In the Admin Console, navigate to ADMIN, Mobile Device Management.

3. In the Tasks list, click Set Mobile Device Management Authority.

4. Select the Use Microsoft Intune To Manage My Mobile Devices check box and then click Yes to use Microsoft Intune to manage mobile devices.

Create a default device enrollment profile

Now that Microsoft Intune is configured to manage mobile devices, you need to create the default device enrollment profile that will manage how newly enrolled devices are pre-assigned to a group in the Microsoft Intune Admin Console.

Follow these steps to create the default device enrollment profile based on the information you prepared during the planning phase:

1. Ensure you are still signed in to the Microsoft Intune Admin Console with administrator permissions.

2. In the Admin Console, navigate to Policy, Corporate Device Enrollment.

3. In the Tasks list, click Add.

4. Enter a policy name and description.

5. Because at least initially you will not prompt for user affinity for iOS devices, select No User Affinity under the Enrollment Details section.

6. Select the group name that newly enrolled devices will automatically be assigned to that you created as part of the planning phase.

7. Select the Save Profile option to complete the default enrollment profile. If this is the first enrollment profile that you have created, it will automatically be set as the default policy. If there is more than one enrollment policy listed, be sure that you use the Set As Default option to make the enrollment policy you have just created as the default.

Customize the Company Portal

The next step in preparing the service is to customize the Company Portal to provide Blue Yonder Airlines employees with support information and to present a streamlined, company-branded experience.

Use these steps to customize the Company Portal for your end-users:

1. Ensure you are still signed in to the Microsoft Intune Admin Console with administrator permissions.

2. Navigate to Admin, Company Portal.

3. Enter the appropriate information gathered during your planning in the Specify Company Name, Company Contact Information And Privacy Statement section:

   - Company Name
   - IT Department Contact Name
   - IT Department Phone Number
   - IT Department Email Address

- Additional Information
- Company Privacy Statement URL

4. In the Specify A Website That Users Can Contact For Support section, provide the tech support website information that your users will select when they need help:
   - Support Website URL (Not Displayed)
   - Website Name (Displayed To User)

5. The Customization section is where you will use the logo files you collected during the planning phase to company-brand the Company Portal for your users, as shown in Figure 6-6.
   - Select a theme color (blue, red, orange, green, or purple).
   - Browse to select the logo that will be used when the Company Portal background is white.
   - Browse to select a second logo that will be used when the Company Portal uses your selected color scheme. Here you can also choose to display the company name next to the logo.
   - Finally, choose a background for the Windows 8 Company Portal app to use (default or white).

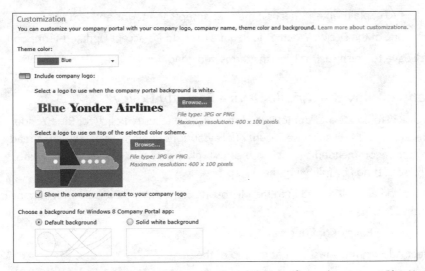

FIGURE 6-6 The Company Portal Customization options configured to support Blue Yonder Airlines company branding

6. The last step of configuring the Company Portal is to click the Microsoft Intune Company Portal link (*https://portal.manage.microsoft.com*) from the Microsoft Intune Company Portal URLs section to review your changes and ensure they are displayed correctly. Don't worry if the customizations don't immediately appear; these updates might take a few minutes to take effect.

Customize usage terms and conditions

With the Company Portal fully customized for your users, your next step is to modify the terms and conditions that you will require all Blue Yonder Airlines employees who will enroll devices into management to agree to before allowing them access to the Company Portal or corporate email.

> **TIP** The easiest way to do this is to simply copy and paste the terms and conditions text from the document you obtained from HR and Legal during the planning phase.

Use these steps to customize the Company Portal for your end-users:

1. While still signed in to the Microsoft Intune Admin Console with administrator permissions, navigate to Admin, Company Portal, Terms And Conditions.

2. Select the Require Users To Accept Company Terms And Conditions Before Using The Company Portal check box.

3. Enter the required terms and conditions information:
   - Title
   - Text for terms
   - Text to explain what it means if the user accepts the terms and conditions

4. Select one of the Decide Whether To Require Users To Re-accept Updated Terms options.

5. Click Save to finish customizing the terms and conditions.

Create and deploy the Mobile Device Security Policy

Your next task is to create and deploy the Mobile Device Security Policy for Blue Yonder Airlines. Because the Mobile Device Security Policy options you have selected are already covered by the recommended settings, you can simply create and deploy a policy with recommended settings by following these steps:

1. Ensure you are still signed in to the Microsoft Intune Admin Console with administrator permissions.

2. Navigate to Policy, Configuration Policies.

3. Select Add from the tasks list at the top of the page.

4. In the Create a New Policy dialog box, expand Common Mobile Device Settings

5. Select the Mobile Device Security Policy option and the Create And Deploy A Policy With The Recommended Settings option.

6. Click Create Policy. This will create the recommended Mobile Device Security Policy and name it Mobile Device Security Policy followed by the creation date and time.

7. In the Select The Groups To Which You Want To Deploy This Policy dialog box, select All Users, Add and then click OK to close the deployment dialog box. This completes the policy creation and deployment process.

Create and deploy email profile configuration policies

While still in the Configuration Policies node of the Policy workspace, now is a good time to create the email profile configuration policies to support Blue Yonder Airlines employees. Because you will support Android, iOS, and Windows devices, you will need to create three separate policies and deploy them to the All Users group to ensure your users receive the appropriate email profile policy setting regardless of the type of device they use to access email.

Follow these steps to create an email profile configuration policy to enable Blue Yonder Airlines users to access corporate email hosted by Exchange Online (Exchange ActiveSync host name *outlook.office365.com* and account name *Blue Yonder Airlines Email Profile*):

1. While still signed in to the Microsoft Intune Admin Console with administrator permissions, navigate to Policy, Configuration Policies.

2. Select Add from the tasks list at the top of the page to open the Create A New Policy dialog box.

3. Create and deploy email profile configuration policies for each mobile device type:

   - **Android Devices**   Expand Android, select Email Profile For Samsung KNOX Standard (4.0 And Later), and then click Create Policy. Enter the required information and click Save Policy. Click Yes in the Deploy Policy dialog box and deploy it to the All Users group.

   - **iOS Devices**   Expand iOS, select Email Profile (iOS 5 And Later), and then click Create Policy. Enter the required information and click Save Policy. Click Yes in the Deploy Policy dialog box and deploy it to the All Users group.

   - **Windows Phone Devices**   Expand Windows, select Email Profile (Windows Phone 8 And Later), and then click Create Policy. Enter the required information and click Save Policy. Click Yes in the Deploy Policy dialog box and deploy it to the All Users group.

Compliance policies

Now that you have established your MDM setting baselines using configuration policies, you need to ensure that those devices remain compliant with your recommended settings. It is a good idea to refer back to your Mobile Device Security Policy documentation as you create the compliance policy because you will want to use the compliance policy to enforce many of those same settings.

As the enterprise administrator for Blue Yonder Airlines, you will need to take the following actions to create and deploy the compliance policy for your organization:

1. While still signed in to the Microsoft Intune Admin Console with administrator permissions, navigate to Policy, Compliance Policies.

2. Select Add from the tasks list at the top of the page to open the Create Policy dialog box.

3. In the General section, give the compliance policy a name and description (optional).

4. Next, you can decide if you will configure all possible compliance settings or just the ones recommended for you. Because the recommended settings cover the basic Mobile Device Security Policy settings you have configured, you can safely ignore that switch for now. Later, you might want to come back and adjust some settings to further tighten security and feature functionality on BYOD devices in use.

> **TIP** Ensure that you configure the remaining compliance setting rules in the following sections to match what you have defined in the mobile device security settings.

5. You can accept the defaults in the Password section because those settings match what you have in the Mobile Device Security Policy.

6. The only setting in the Advanced Passwords Settings section that you need to enable and configure is the Required Password Type setting. Set this to match what you have in the Mobile Device Security Policy (Alphanumeric or Numeric).

7. Configure the Require Encryption On Mobile Devices setting to match the Mobile Device Security Policy setting (recommended yes).

8. Because company security policy is to not allow this, enable the Jailbreak option to verify that devices are not jailbroken or rooted.

9. Because you will be managing the email profiles for Blue Yonder Airlines employees, you can enable the Email Profiles option to ensure that email accounts are managed by Microsoft Intune (iOS 6+ only). After you enable this option, you will need to use the drop-down list to select the iOS email profile configuration policy you created earlier to preconfigure Blue Yonder Airlines email access for your users.

10. Click Save Policy.

11. In the Deploy Policy dialog box, click Yes to manage the deployment of the compliance policy.

12. In the Select The Groups To Which You Want To Deploy This Policy dialog box, select All Users, Add, and then click OK to close the deployment dialog box. This completes the policy creation and deployment process.

Conditional access policies

The last policy that needs to be addressed before you can turn your focus to enrolling devices is the Conditional Access Policy. Remember, this is the policy that will restrict access to corporate email to only those devices managed by Microsoft Intune and in compliance with Blue Yonder Airlines company policies that you have just previously defined.

There are several prerequisites that must be in place to create and deploy this policy. You have already identified an Active Directory security group that you will apply the policy to during planning and you have also just deployed a compliance policy, but before creating the

Conditional Access Policy, you still need to set up the Microsoft Intune Online Connector for Online Exchange. This connector allows you to discover and manage mobile devices connecting to the Exchange Online instance for Blue Yonder Airlines that are otherwise unmanaged. To do that, follow these steps:

1. Ensure you are still signed in to the Microsoft Intune Admin Console with administrator permissions to both Microsoft Intune *and* to your Exchange Online instance and then navigate to Admin, Mobile Device Management, Microsoft Exchange and select the Set Up A Connection To Exchange Environment option.

2. Select the Set Up Service To Service Connector option.

3. You should see a message similar to the one shown in Figure 6-7. Click OK to continue.

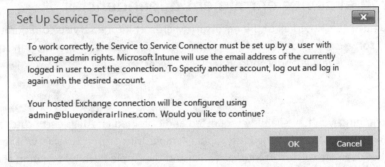

FIGURE 6-7 The Set Up Service To Service Connector dialog box

4. In the Admin Console, you should now select the Run Quick Sync option to immediately start the synchronization process between Microsoft Intune and Exchange Online.

5. Navigate to Groups, All Devices, All Mobile Devices, All Exchange ActiveSync Managed Devices to verify that the synchronization is working. It might take a few minutes, but eventually you should see devices listed there that are currently being managed only by Exchange ActiveSync.

> **TIP** These devices will also be the ones blocked from accessing Exchange email until they are managed by Microsoft Intune based on the Conditional Access Policy you are about to deploy. It might be a good time to alert affected users that this change is coming and give them the opportunity to self-enroll their devices before their email access is blocked.

With all of the prerequisites out of the way, you are now ready to create and deploy the Blue Yonder Airlines Conditional Access Policy using the following steps:

1. Ensure you are still signed in to the Microsoft Intune Admin Console with administrator permissions and navigate to Policy, Conditional Access, Exchange Online Policy.

2. Select the Block Email Apps From Accessing Exchange Online If The Device Is Noncompliant option.

3. In the Targeted Groups section, search for and add the security group that you have previously created during planning that includes the users that you want to apply this policy to.

4. In the Exempted Groups section, search for and add the security group that you have previously created during planning that includes the users that you do *not* want to apply this policy to.

5. In the Unsupported Platforms section, select an option to either block or allow access to email on devices that are not supported by Microsoft Intune. In this case, select the option to allow access.

6. Click Save to complete the Conditional Access Policy creation and deployment process.

Satisfy external device enrollment dependencies

At this point you have completed all of the necessary Microsoft Intune service configurations, but there are still some external dependencies that must be addressed before you can successfully enroll and manage iOS and Windows mobile devices.

iOS devices

As part of your planning, you have already requested and obtained an APNs certificate. That certificate must now be uploaded to the Blue Yonder Airlines Microsoft Intune service to create the trust between the Microsoft Intune service and the Apple Push Notification service to interact with the iOS devices that you want to manage.

To prepare your Microsoft Intune service to support iOS devices, you must plan for, and complete, the following actions:

1. While signed in to the Microsoft Intune Admin Console with administrator permissions, navigate to Admin, Mobile Device Management, iOS.

2. Select the Upload An APNs Certificate option to open the Upload An APNs Certificate page.

3. Select the option to Upload The APNs Certificate and then browse to the .pem file that you previously downloaded during the planning process. You will also need to provide the Apple ID used to obtain the certificate. When you are ready to upload the APNs certificate, the dialog box should look similar to Figure 6-8.

FIGURE 6-8 The Upload The APNs Certificate dialog box

4. To verify that these steps were completed successfully, look for a message displayed in the Microsoft Intune Admin Console notifying you that the service is ready for iOS enrollment along with details about your APNs certificate.

Windows devices

Because you have previously created a CNAME record with your domain registrar to enable Windows devices to locate the enrollment server, all you need to do at this point is verify that the DNS zone file updates have completed and that Windows devices will be able to successfully locate the enrollment server when users try to enroll their devices. Follow these steps:

1. Back in the Microsoft Intune Admin Portal with admin rights, navigate to Admin, Mobile Device Management, Windows, enter your public domain name in the Step 1 text box area, and select the Test Auto-Detection option. You should receive a message stating that the test was successful.

2. Now navigate to Admin, Mobile Device Management, Windows Phone, enter your public domain name in the Step 1 text box area, and select the Test Auto-Detection option.

3. You should receive another message stating that the test was successful, similar to Figure 6-9.

FIGURE 6-9 A successful name resolution test for Windows devices to access the enrollment server for Blue Yonder Airlines

Windows Phone 8.0

Because you have already done all the hard work and preparation for supporting Windows Phone 8.0 devices in the planning phase, all that remains is to upload the signed Windows Phone 8.0 Company Portal app into the Microsoft Intune service. Follow these steps:

1. In the Microsoft Intune Admin Console, navigate to Admin, Mobile Device Management, Windows Phone.

2. Select the option to Upload Signed App.

3. Sign in to the Add Software wizard using an account with administrator permissions.

4. Use the Browse button to find and select your signed Company Portal app (.xap file).

5. Clear the option to use the sample Symantec code-signing certificate[2].

6. Upload and complete the wizard to deploy the signed Windows Phone 8.0 Company Portal app.

> **TIP** At this point you have completed all the necessary service configurations and pre-requisites required for enrolling mobile devices! To double-check, navigate to the Admin, Mobile Device Management page and ensure that you see green check marks for each mobile device platform that you want to support.

Enrolling devices

As an administrator, you can assign device-enrollment managers who will be authorized by the service to enroll more than five devices—the device limit normally set by Microsoft Intune. This role is useful when enrolling several company-owned devices into management with Microsoft Intune. Another bulk enrollment option for iOS devices is to use the Apple Configurator tool running on a Mac computer to bulk enroll company-owned iOS devices. However, in the following BYOD scenario, users will enroll up to five of their own personal devices into management with Microsoft Intune using the Company Portal app or a mobile device setting.

The following sections describe the enrollment process for each of the devices supported by Microsoft Intune:

- iOS
- Android
- Windows devices (Windows Phone 8.0, Windows Phone 8.1, and Windows 8.1 computers enrolled as devices).

You can check BYOD self-enrollment progress and verify that each of your users' devices enrolls successfully by looking in the custom device group that you specified in the default enrollment profile to see devices as they are enrolled.

Enrolling iOS devices

The process to enroll iOS devices is the same for both iPhones and iPads. Because the APNs certificate is already provisioned, users can download the iOS Company Portal app and follow these simple instructions to get their devices enrolled into management:

---

[2]   When evaluating Microsoft Intune, you can use the support tool for Microsoft Intune trial management of Windows Phone; it is a download that includes a Windows Phone 8 Company Portal app and several sample programs that have been code-signed using a sample Symantec code-signing certificate. Use the production-ready, code-signed Windows Phone 8.0 Company Portal app that you created during the planning phase. You can learn more about the sample tools for Microsoft Intune trials at *http://www.microsoft.com/en-us/download/details.aspx?id=39079*.

1. On the iOS device, open the Apple App Store and search for the Microsoft Intune Company Portal app.

2. Install the app and then open it.

3. Sign in to the Company Portal using your corporate credentials. As soon as you enter your name, the page should be redirected to your custom AD FS sign-in page, similar to what is shown in Figure 6-10.

FIGURE 6-10 The customized Blue Yonder Airlines AD FS sign-in page, as seen on an iPad

4. The Device Enrollment dialog box will appear. Review the details about device enrollment and then click Enroll to continue.

5. Click Install to install the management profile for your company (Blue Yonder Airlines) on the iOS device utilizing the trust protected by the APNs certificate.

6. Review the Warning dialog box that describes administrator actions that will be enabled by installing this management profile and then click Install to continue.

7. In the Remote Management dialog box, tap Trust to verify that you trust the source of the trust to remotely manage the device.

8. When profile installation completes, tap Done to open the Company Portal app. Because you have previously configured the option to enforce acceptance of the terms and conditions, those terms and conditions will now be displayed and they must be accepted by tapping Done, as shown in Figure 6-11.

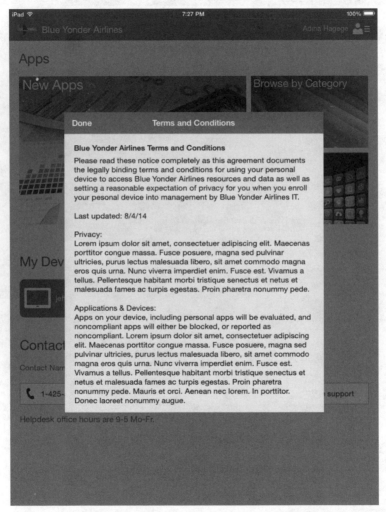

FIGURE 6-11 The customized Blue Yonder Airlines Terms And Conditions, as seen on an iPad

9. The device is now enrolled and will begin synchronizing with the Microsoft Intune service to apply policies, including pre-configuring the email profile to connect to Exchange Online, and verify compliance with the configuration policies that you

previously created and deployed. Any applications that have been deployed to the user and the device type she is using will be displayed as well as any Company Portal customizations you have made, as shown in Figure 6-12.

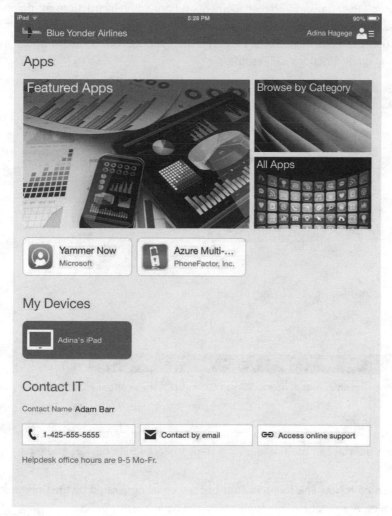

FIGURE 6-12 The customized Company Portal as seen by a signed-in Blue Yonder Airlines employee on her iPad

Enrolling Android devices

The process to enroll an Android device into management with Microsoft Intune is very similar to that used to enroll an iOS device, but in this case, end users need to install the Company Portal app from the Google Play Store.

In this example, you can see how conditional access policies are used to ensure that all devices accessing corporate email are managed by Microsoft Intune and are in compliance with administrator-defined policies. This might be the way many of your users discover the need to enroll their devices if they have previously configured corporate email on their devices. If that is the case, they will receive an email similar to the one shown in Figure 6-13, informing them of the need to enroll their devices into management and providing instructions for doing so. The email is the same regardless of which devices they are using, but it will be the last email they receive on that particular device until they are in compliance with company policy, at which time normal email functions will resume.

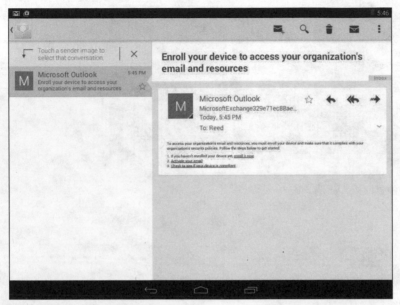

FIGURE 6-13 A user being notified that he must enroll his Android device into management to regain email access

Users who have been denied access to Exchange email on their Android devices via conditional access policies can use the following steps to enroll their devices and regain access to email:

1. Click the Enroll It Now link found in Step 1 of the email generated by the Conditional Access policy. A webpage will be opened on the device.

2. Select the only option available on that webpage to Get The App. You might be prompted at this point by a Complete Action dialog box. If that happens, select the Play Store to complete the task.

> **TIP** Alternatively, if the user just wants to enroll his Android device, he can search for the Microsoft Intune Company Portal app from the Google Play Store and follow the remaining steps.

3. The Microsoft Intune Company Portal app will be displayed on the screen. Click Install to install it on the device.

4. The Company Portal app permissions are displayed and must be accepted before continuing.

5. Once installed, click Open to launch the Company Portal app and then click Next to begin the device enrollment process.

6. The user is prompted to sign in and should be automatically redirected to the customized company AD FS sign-in page, similar to what is shown in Figure 6-14.

FIGURE 6-14 The customized Blue Yonder Airlines AD FS sign-in page, as seen on an Android device.

7. Once signed in, the custom company terms and conditions will be displayed to the user. Click Accept to accept the usage terms and conditions.

8. The device will prompt you to activate the device administrator to enable the Company Portal app to perform administrative actions on the device. Click Activate to continue.

The device will now complete the enrollment process and the apps and company resources available to the user on Android devices will now be shown, as seen in Figure 6-15.

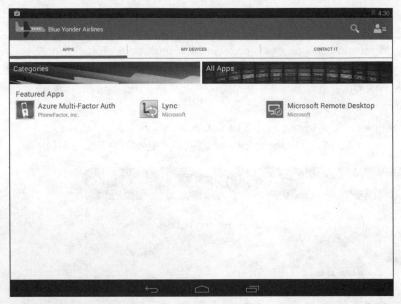

FIGURE 6-15 The customized Company Portal as seen by a signed-in Blue Yonder Airlines employee on his Android tablet

Enrolling Windows devices

The process for enrolling Windows devices is also pretty straightforward, but the steps vary according to the type of Windows device that you are enrolling.

The following sections explain how to enroll some of the various supported Windows devices your users might be using.

Enrolling Windows Phone 8.0 devices

Now is when all the hard work to code-sign the Windows Phone 8.0 Company Portal app pays off. Because you have already code-signed and uploaded the app to the Microsoft Intune service, it will be available for your users to install by following these simple steps:

1. On the Windows Phone 8.0 device, open Settings and then scroll down and tap Company Apps.

2. Review the information about the significance of adding a company account to the device and then tap Add Account.

3. Provide company credentials and select Sign In.

   At this point, the device will begin searching for the enrollment server and for the settings that should be applied to the device.

> **TIP** This is when the device will be searching for the enrollment server based on the CNAME DNS record you created earlier to direct it to manage.microsoft.com.

4. When the account is successfully added, the device will now be enrolled into management. The Windows Phone 8.0 Company Portal app can now be installed by selecting the Install Company App Or Hub option and then tapping Done, as shown in Figure 6-16.

FIGURE 6-16 A user installing the signed Windows Phone 8.0 Company Portal app during device enrollment

Enrolling Windows Phone 8.1

The process for enrolling a Windows Phone 8.1 device is very similar to that used by both Android and iOS devices. Users simply need to install the Company Portal app and sign in to enroll their devices using these steps:

1. On the Windows Phone 8.1 device, open the Microsoft Store and search for the Microsoft Intune Company Portal app.

2. Install the app and then open it.

3. Sign in with company credentials after being redirected to the custom AD FS sign-in page.

4. Read and accept the custom company terms and conditions by clicking Accept.

5. At this point you will be granted access to the Company Portal and any Windows device apps available to you, as shown in Figure 6-17. However, the device will not be enrolled yet.

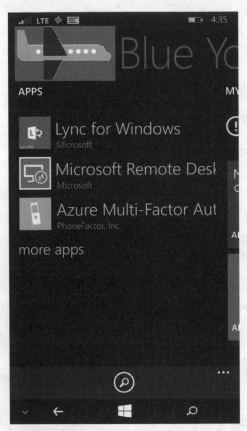

FIGURE 6-17 A Blue Yonder Airlines employee signed in to the Company Portal on her Windows 8.1 phone

6. To enroll the device, swipe over to the My Devices screen and tap the Tap To Enroll This Device option.

7. On the workplace screen, tap Add Account.

8. Enter the same credentials used to sign in to the Company Portal on the workplace email address page and tap Sign In. After being redirected to the custom AD FS sign-in page, enter the password for the account and tap Sign In, as shown in Figure 6-18.

FIGURE 6-18 The customized Blue Yonder Airlines AD FS sign-in page, as seen on a Windows 8.1 Phone

9. The device will begin searching for the enrollment server and other account settings. Once found, the device is enrolled and tapping Done completes the process.

10. You can verify or change the enrollment settings on this device from the workplace page in the phone settings.

Enrolling Windows 8.1 computers as devices

Windows 8.1 computers can be managed by Microsoft Intune as either managed computers or enrolled devices. To manage Windows 8.1 computers as managed computers, administrators can install the Microsoft Intune agent on the computers manually, through Group Policy, or even as part of a computer operating system image.

However, in this example, users self-enroll their computers as devices from the Company Portal website using the following steps. Each computer that they enroll will then automatically be linked to their user accounts.

1. A user with administrative rights on the computer logs on to the computer and then uses Internet Explorer to browse to the Company Portal website at *https://portal.manage.microsoft.com/.*

2. The user logs into the Company Portal website using company credentials, which automatically redirect her to the custom AD FS sign-in page.

3. The custom terms and conditions are displayed and must be accepted before continuing.

4. When the Company Portal is displayed, the user clicks the Add Device option from the task list at the top of the screen, as shown in Figure 6-19.

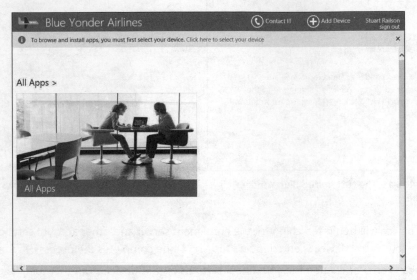

FIGURE 6-19 A Blue Yonder Airlines employee signed in to the Company Portal website on her Windows 8.1 computer

5. Click the Download Software button to download the Microsoft Intune software to the local computer.

6. At the bottom of the web browser, select the Run Microsoft_Intune_Setup.exe option. At this point, the Microsoft Intune client software will be downloaded and run on the local computer.

7. Click Finish to complete the Microsoft Intune Setup Wizard, as shown in Figure 6-20.

8. After a few minutes, the Microsoft Intune computer client software will complete installation, which makes the Microsoft Intune Center and Company Portal options available from the taskbar.

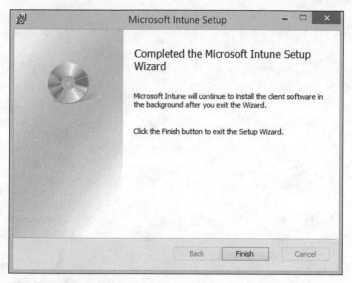

FIGURE 6-20 The last page of the Microsoft Intune Setup wizard

This completes the Windows 8.1 computer enrollment process. With the Microsoft Intune client software installed, administrators can remotely take actions to manage application deployment, software update installation, Endpoint Protection to defend against malware, and remote assistance options (on supported operating systems).

## Chapter 7

Data access and protection

At this point you have already implemented the identity solution that will be used for your mobile workforce. You also implemented device management giving you control of user-owned devices as well as company-owned devices. While these are critical components of Enterprise Mobility Suite (EMS), there is still one more pillar that must be addressed: data access and protection. Since data is at the center of your solution, and ultimately companies that are embracing mobility want to keep their data secure, it is vital to understand the ramifications of this last pillar before implementing it.

This chapter discusses how to leverage some built-in capabilities available in Windows Server 2012 R2 in combination with the last component of EMS, called Azure Rights Management Services (RMS), to build the proper data access and protection solution to embrace mobility.

Leveraging on-premises resources

When you are moving to a model where users will be accessing corporate information from different locations using different devices, it is important that security is not only part of the solution but that it is actually embedded in the data itself. The goal is to have security controls in place that can be attached to the data and, regardless of the data location, those controls can still be applicable. Imagine circulating a Microsoft Word document that contains confidential information about the company's next generation of products to many users on various different devices. The chances of data breach will increase as the number of users and devices increases; however, you can mitigate this risk.

The Windows operating system includes multiple capabilities that can and should be used for data protection. As is described in Chapter 2, you must apply a defense-in-depth strategy for data protection and part of this strategy is to leverage capabilities that are natively available in Windows Server and Windows client devices. Throughout this section of the book, you will learn about these key capabilities that are natively available in Windows that should also be leveraged as part of your enterprise mobility strategy for data protection.

After you finish identifying these capabilities, you will learn how Azure RMS should be used to enhance data access and protection for your enterprise mobility adoption.

Windows Server Dynamic Access Control

A big part of protecting data is understanding how to translate business intent with proper use of the technology to reflect that intent. If the company determines that documents containing financial data should be read only by members of the Finance department, that's the business intent for that particular data access. While this is the main intent, it can be extended to a more granular set of requirements. For example, the company might also say that members of the Finance department must only be able to access documents based on the physical location of those members. This feature can be very important for companies that have a worldwide presence and have users accessing information from different locations.

> **MORE INFO** One example of use of this feature for compliance purposes is the Safe Harbor scenario, where the data falls under the US-European Union Safe Harbor regulation. For more information about this scenario, visit *http://aka.ms/dacsafeharbor*.

Dynamic Access Control (DAC) enables IT administrators to perform data governance across file servers to control who can access information and it enables administrators to audit who has accessed information. To perform this task, DAC uses a Windows authorization and audit engine that can process conditional expressions and central policies. It also leverages Kerberos authentication support for user claims and device claims. While this feature was first introduced in Windows Server 2012, it leverages capabilities that were first introduced in Windows Server 2008 R2, such as File Classification Infrastructure (FCI) and conditional access permission entry. The key factor in Windows Server 2012 R2 is that FCI is claims-aware; this allows FCI to present resource properties as classification properties.

> **NOTE** What is a claim? A claim is information a trusted source makes about an entity. The security identifier (SID) of a user or computer and the department classification of a file are all examples of a claim.

IT administrators use central access policies to create access policies that apply to Windows Server 2012 file servers that are using Group Policy. Each central access policy object can contain one or more central access rules. These rules are used to translate the policies you require into expressions. All rules created in the Central Access Policy page are stored in Windows Server Active Directory, which enables the organization to have a centralized approach to manage authorization on Windows Server 2012 file servers. To plan central access policy deployment, refer to *http://technet.microsoft.com/en-us/library/hh831366.aspx#BKMK_1_2*.

> **TIP** If you are not familiar with DAC, you can watch the demonstration shown at *http://technet.microsoft.com/en-us/video/dynamic-access-control-demo-walkthrough.aspx*.

Conditional Access Control

Chapter 6 describes the different levels of Conditional Access Control you can create via Microsoft Intune. From the DAC perspective, when you create access rules, what you are really doing is creating a set of conditions that will allow access to certain information. In previous versions of Windows, the mechanism to allow or deny access to resources is determined by searching for the permission entry's trustee security identifier (SID) within the security principal's access token. When the SID is present, Windows evaluates the permission and verifies whether that permission entry is applicable to the user and, if so, Windows includes that permission entry along with all other applicable permission entries when evaluating access.

Starting in Windows Server 2012 and Windows 8, another layer of decision was introduced to evaluate conditional expressions. Considering that there are multiple conditional expressions, the results of all conditional expressions must evaluate to *true* for Windows to consider the entry for this permission and apply the proper authorization. Table 7-1 shows how this looks when compared to the traditional access-control entries.

TABLE 7-1 Additional security with Conditional Access Control

Principal	Permission type	NTFS security permissions	Conditional Access	Inherited from
Jeff	Deny	Full control Modify Read & execute Read Write	None	None
Yuri	Allow	Read & execute Read	User.Department=="IT"	C:\ITDocs

Using conditional expression for auditing

While controlling the access to data is important, part of your mobility strategy is to monitor a user's activities. Auditing resource usage is a critical element of an overall security plan. By using auditing, IT administrators can configure Windows to write events that relate to a specific action to the Windows event log. IT administrators can configure Windows to write an event when the action results in a success or when the action fails. Windows evaluates an audit entry's applicability by considering the audit entry's trustee, the action, that action's result, and the conditional expression. When conditional expressions are used for auditing purposes, Windows evaluates all expressions in an audit entry to determine if the audit entry is applicable. Just like conditional expressions in permission entries, the conditional expression in an audit entry must evaluate to true for the audit entry to apply.

Web Application Proxy

For companies that are adopting enterprise mobility, it is important to balance which applications will be a fully cloud-based apps by leveraging Software-as-a-Service (SaaS) apps and which on-premises apps will be available for remote consumption. As you learned in Chapter 3 and Chapter 4, the use of hybrid identity with Azure AD Premium allows you to easily integrate with SaaS apps; however, the reality is that most companies have production apps on-premises. In many cases, these production apps will need to be accessed by mobile users.

In Windows Server 2012, a featured called Web Application Proxy was introduced to enable IT Administrators to securely publish applications that are located on-premises. Ideally, you should always deploy Web Application Proxy in conjunction with Active Directory Federation Services (AD FS) to enable conditional access and also Single Sign-On (SSO) capabilities. In Chapter 3 and Chapter 4, you installed Web Application Proxy as part of the Azure AD Connect Wizard configuration, but this role can be installed separately using Server Manager.

> **MORE INFO** For more information about Web Application Proxy, read the article at *http://technet.microsoft.com/en-us/library/dn584113.aspx*. For more information about AD FS Conditional Access Control, read the article at *http://technet.microsoft.com/en-us/library/dn280936.aspx*.

Publishing on-premises apps

When you use Web Application Proxy to publish on-premises apps in combination with AD FS, the typical infrastructure is comprised of the AD FS located inside the boundaries of the corporate network, and the Web Application Proxy, which is also the Active Directory Federation Services Proxy, located at the perimeter of the corporate network. The Web Application Proxy directs all authentication traffic to the AD FS in the internal network and provisions for certificate-based authentication in particular. This means that the Web Application Proxy terminates the traffic and initiates a new request to the published applications. By performing this task, the Web Application Proxy acts as a session-level buffer between the external device and published applications. This behavior adds another layer of security since the user accessing the published application will not have direct access to the application itself; instead, the user accesses the application through Web Application Proxy. Figure 7-1 shows an example of a typical topology.

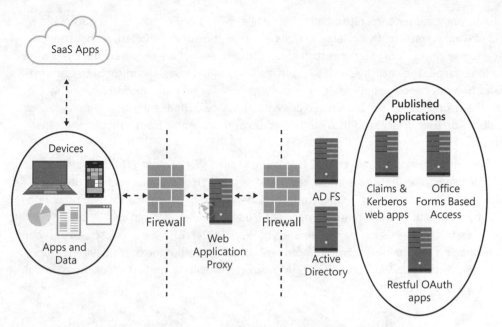

FIGURE 7-1 Typical topology for publishing on-premises apps using Web Application Proxy

> **TIP** Windows Server Technical Preview introduced the capability to enable Preauthentication for HTTP Basic application publishing. For more information about this new feature, read the TechNet article at *http://technet.microsoft.com/en-us/library/dn765483.aspx*.

Device registration

Web Application Proxy is also used in scenarios where mobile users must register their devices before accessing internal resources. The Device Registration Service is integrated with the AD FS Server Role. When this capability is configured in the AD FS server, the only task that needs to be performed in the Web Application Proxy is to update the configuration using the Windows PowerShell command Update-WebApplicationProxyDeviceRegistration. You also need to register a public Domain Name System (DNS) CName for deviceregistration.

Protecting data at rest at the user device location using work folders

The likelihood of data leakage with mobility increases because mobility increases the threat landscape, but if correctly planned, it is possible to reduce this likelihood by adding countermeasures that will reduce the risk. One of the most challenging aspects of enterprise mobility is to properly deliver corporate data to users while maintaining control of this information and making it consistently available to users across all their devices. Often, mobile users tend to use cloud storage services such as OneDrive or even share corporate documents via personal email. The challenge with this is that a corporation loses all control of the information when this happens, both from a risk point of view (for example, the information falling into the wrong hands) or from a compliance point of view (with the information only being available on user devices and thus not backed up or discoverable from a regulatory compliance stance).

By using the Windows Server 2012 R2 featured called Work Folders, IT administrators enforce users to securely store and access work files on personal computers and devices in addition to corporate PCs. IT administrators will be able to maintain control over corporate data by storing the files on centrally managed file servers; they also can specify security policies to instruct user PCs and devices to encrypt Work Folders and use a lock screen password. By leveraging this built-in feature, you can protect data at rest at the user's device location. If the user is setting up Work Folders using Windows 8, he will be notified about these policies, as shown in Figure 7-2.

> **MORE INFO** You can read more about Work Folders in the TechNet article at *http://technet.microsoft.com/en-us/library/dn265974.aspx*. You can also use Work Folders in Windows 7; see the TechNet article at *blogs.technet.com/b/filecab/archive/2014/04/24/work-folders-for-windows-7.aspx*.

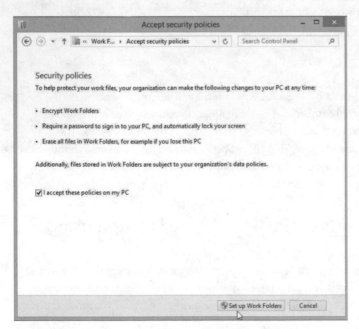

FIGURE 7-2 The notification that appears when a user is setting up work folders using Windows 8

The infrastructure to support this functionality is shown in Figure 7-3. It enables both mobile users coming from outside of the corporate network and users who are using domain-joined computers located on-premises.

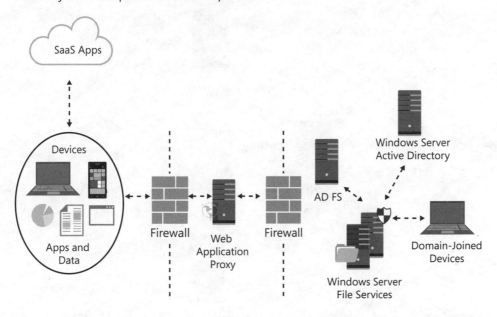

FIGURE 7-3 Infrastructure to support work folders for internal and external users

Active Directory Rights Management Services

For companies that have already invested in an on-premises infrastructure and want to keep managing their data classification under this infrastructure, they can use the Active Directory AD RMS. AD RMS is designed for companies that need to protect sensitive and proprietary information, such as financial reports, product specifications, customer data, and confidential email messages. AD RMS consists of modules that are located on the server as well as on the client side. The server component composed by multiple web services that run on an Internet Information Server (IIS). The module located in the client can be run on either a client or a server operating system. The module located on the client side contains functions that enable an application to encrypt and decrypt content, retrieve templates and revocation lists, acquire licenses and certificates from a server, and many other related tasks.

You can integrate the DAC feature that was previously described in this chapter with AD RMS to enhance your security by applying data classification for mobile users while they are accessing resources located on-premises. By using content scanning and classification policies, the AD RMS Server is able to verify if the content that is being accessed has rights management policies that must be applied to it and if there are it will execute these policies. You can also perform this task in a folder located in the file server, which can also be the location where the users that are storing their Work Folders data to access from their devices. The infrastructure for this solution is presented in the diagram shown in Figure 7-4.

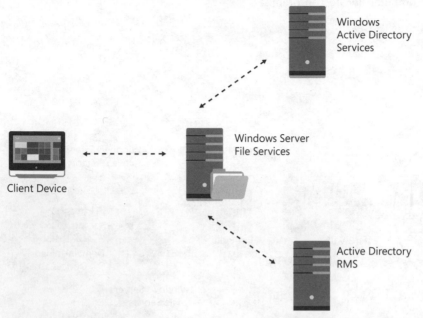

FIGURE 7-4 Infrastructure to support the integration between DAC, Work Folders and AD RMS

> **MORE INFO** For more information about AD RMS, read the TechNet article at *http://technet.microsoft.com/en-us/library/hh831554.aspx.*

Leveraging built-in client capabilities for data protection

As explained in Chapter 1, it is important to protect data at rest, not only on the servers located on-premises or in the cloud but also on the user's device. In Chapter 5 and Chapter 6, you learned some device management capabilities to protect data at rest on the user's device; however, you should also leverage built-in features in the client's platform to enhance this data protection. Some security features available in Windows 8.1 are able to distinguish corporate data from user data. By leveraging Windows technologies to encrypt and control access to corporate data, you can enhance your enterprise mobility experience for devices using Windows operating system.

Mobile devices using the Windows Phone 8.1 operating system will natively have device encryption enabled based on BitLocker technology. This technology is used to encrypt the internal storage using Advanced Encryption Standard (AES) 128-bit encryption. By leveraging this capability, IT administrators can certify that the data is always protected from unauthorized users, even when unauthorized users have physical control of the phones. Companies that are using Exchange ActiveSync Mailbox Policies can enable the Require Device Encryption policy to prevent users from disabling device encryption on their devices.

> **MORE INFO**   For more information about what's new in security for Windows 8.1, read the TechNet article at *http://technet.microsoft.com/en-us/library/dn344918.aspx*. For more information about Windows phone security, visit *http://curah.microsoft.com/192722/ windows-phone-security*.

Azure RMS

Azure RMS comes with EMS to assist IT administrators to protect sensitive information from unauthorized access, and control how this information is used. Azure RMS requires an Azure AD directory, which you can create (refer to Chapter 4 for more details) because EMS provides you with a subscription for Azure AD Premium. Azure RMS uses encryption, identity, and authorization policies to help secure company data located in files and email messages.

Azure RMS is the closest protection of the data because, when you apply an Azure RMS template to the data, the rights stay with the file itself, regardless of where the file is located. This guarantees that the data is protected in place and in flight, in other words: it is protected all the time. IT administrators will remain in control of company data even when the data is shared with those outside of the organization. Although there are many flavors of RMS, the intent of this section is to focus on Azure RMS because this is the one that comes with EMS. (The available subscriptions for RMS are described at *http://technet.microsoft.com/en-us/ library/dn655136.aspx#BKMK_SupportedSubscriptions*.)

The Azure RMS service requires storage for the high-value tenant keys at the core of RMS. The Microsoft Key Management Service (KMS) used by Azure RMS stores these RMS tenant keys in a highly secure manner by using industry-proven, Federal Information Processing Standards (FIPS)-compliant Hardware Security Modules (HSMs)[1]. However, for companies that want to keep control of their keys, they can also use the Bring Your Own Key (BYOK) capability available in Azure RMS. (This functionality will be described in more detail later in this chapter.) Figure 7-5 shows a diagram the components that will be consuming the data protection capability provided by Azure RMS.

---

[1]   Azure RMS uses Thales HSMs to protect tenant keys. For more information, visit *https://www.thales-esecurity. com/msrms/cloud*.

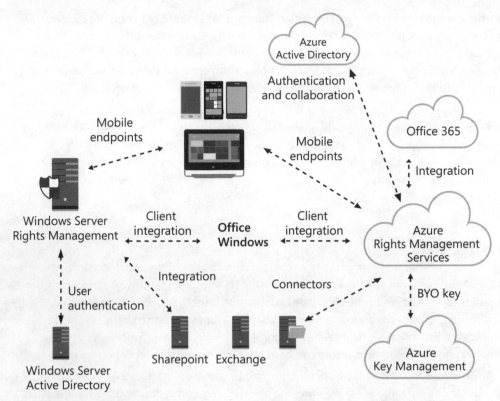

FIGURE 7-5 Azure RMS can be leveraged by on-premises services and also SaaS applications

With Azure RMS, you can protect not only Microsoft Office files but also other types of files, which are called generic files. When a generic file is protected using Azure RMS, an encapsulation is added to the file using pfile (protected file). This means that if the file has the TXT extension, the protected version will have the PTXT extension[2]. Another layer of security is also provided by including the authentication, which is used to verify whether a user is authorized to open the file.

> **IMPORTANT** Applications that understand Rights Management are called RMS-enlightened applications.

While the key focus of Azure RMS is to protect data handled by the end user, you can also integrate Azure RMS with servers located on on-premises servers. For example, if you have an Exchange Server 2013 on-premises server and you want to protect email messages by using Azure RMS, you need to use the Azure RMS connector to act as a communication relay between Exchange Server 2013 on-premises and Azure RMS.

---

[2] To see a list of supported files, visit *http://technet.microsoft.com/en-US/library/d9992e30-f3d1-48d5-aedc-4e721f7d7c25(v=ws.10)#BKMK_SupportFileTypes*.

How Azure RMS works

One of the main concerns that organizations have in using cloud services to encrypt their sensitive data is regarding data integrity and confidentiality. For this reason, it is critical for companies that are adopting EMS to understand that when they use Azure RMS, it does not see or store their data as part of the information protection process. The information itself that you protect using Azure RMS is never sent to or stored in Azure unless you explicitly choose to store in Azure or you use another cloud service that uses Azure storage.

The data that will be protected by Azure RMS is encrypted at the application level and, once it is protected, it includes in the file's header the policy that defines the authorized use for that data. When a protected document is used by a legitimate user or is processed by an authorized service, the data in the document is decrypted and the rights that are defined in the policy are enforced. Figure 7-6 shows how this process occurs for a user who wants to protect a document located in the on-premises file server by leveraging Azure RMS.

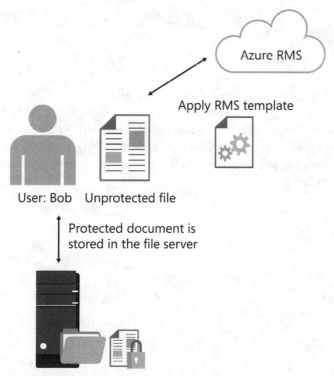

FIGURE 7-6 Azure RMS can be used to protect files located on-premises

MORE INFO For a detailed explanation of this process, read "Walkthrough of how Azure RMS works: First use, content protection, content consumption" at *http://technet.microsoft. com/en-us/library/jj585026.aspx#BKMK_Walkthrough*.

In the particular scenario shown in Figure 7-6, the protection of the file could be simply done by applying one Azure RMS policy that was previously created by the IT administrator and published for the users. Figure 7-7 shows an example of a custom policy called "BYOD Policy" that is available using Microsoft Word after this application retrieves the templates from Azure RMS.

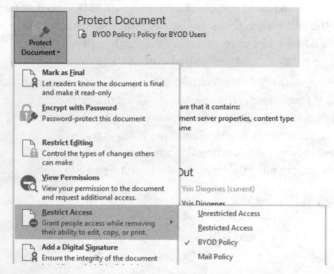

FIGURE 7-7 Document created using Microsoft Word with Azure RMS policy available to protect the data

When another user tries to open this file, she will see that this particular BYOD Policy was applied and this BYOD Policy was previously created with custom settings. When she verifies the permissions by clicking the View Permission button, she will be able to see what privileges she has on this file, as shown in Figure 7-8.

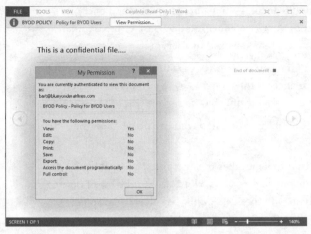

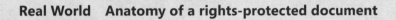

FIGURE 7-8 The user will be able to see what privileges she has to the file once the policies are applied

Real World   Anatomy of a rights-protected document

A zure RMS service works along with the client software to encrypt each document. This allows the protection and rights to travel with the document itself.
The following diagram represents an RMS-aware document.

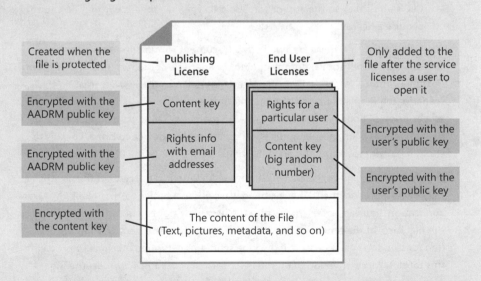

The following is a step-by-step example of how the file is built/encrypted using
Azure RMS:

1. The client creates a random symmetric key (content key).

2. The client takes the body of the document it wants to protect and encrypts it with the content key. It ends up with an encrypted version of the original document, and it still has the content key used to encrypt it.

3. The client has a local copy of the Server Licensor Certificate (SLC) with its public key. It uses this public key to encrypt the content key, which means that this encrypted content key will be readable only by the service whose SLC was used.

4. The client then creates a list of rights expressing who can do what on the document.

5. After creating a list of rights, the client takes the encrypted content key (encrypted with the SLC), the public part of its own CLC, and the list of rights created before, encrypts them with the SLC's public key along with some other information (such as the URL of the Licensing URL that should be used to acquire a license to consume the document), and builds what we call the Publishing License (PL) with them. This PL is then encrypted with the SLC's public key so only the service will be able to decrypt it. The client also takes the private key from the user's Client Licensor Certificate (CLC) and signs the encrypted object.

6. This is embedded into the original content encrypted with the content key to create a protected document. The content key is also stored encrypted with the CLC's public key so the author can also decrypt the content without having to acquire a license.

To work around this, there are two hybrid document formats that are essentially the same as the format above, but the content is a generic container for the encrypted document (much like a .zip file). This format is known as the PFILE format. In this scenario, the Rights Management Sharing App (available on iOS and Android as well as a Windows Phone) acts as the Rights Management (RM) Aware application and decrypts the file for another application on the mobile device to open. For this to work, the user protecting the document must encrypt it in the PFILE format.

The downside to this format is that once the document is decrypted, the user has a fully decrypted document. If everything was kept in a native format of an RM Aware application, you can, for example, give the user view rights without rights to modify the file. Also, at the time of this writing, the Rights Management Sharing Application for Windows must be installed on the sending/encrypting machine to protect in this format. Another variation on the PFILE format is the PPDF format. The Rights Management Sharing Application can use this format to include not only the original protected document but also a PDF rendering of the document. This allows further flexibility in that you don't need the corresponding application to read the document (you will if you actually want to modify it).

Eddie Bowers
Senior Support Escalation Engineer, CSS Azure RMS Support Team

Choosing the right deployment topology

When planning to adopt Azure RMS as part of your enterprise mobility strategy, you must first decide which tenant key topology is best for your company. The option that the company will choose will directly impact not only the adoption but also the maintenance of the cloud service. The available options are:

- Centralized in the cloud topology (Microsoft manages the master key)
- Hybrid topology (company manages the master key)

When you activate an EMS subscription and start using Azure RMS, the default tenant key topology used is fully cloud based. In this topology, Azure RMS generates the tenant key and manages most aspects of the tenant key lifecycle. The advantage of this option is the simplicity of configuration and the low administrative overhead of maintenance. The entire process is transparent for the company; the IT administrator doesn't even know that there is a tenant key in place. In this topology, you simply sign up for Azure RMS and the rest of the entire key-management process is automatically handled by Microsoft. Figure 7-9 shows this topology.

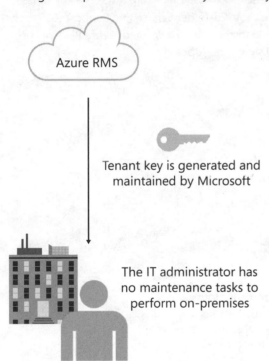

FIGURE 7-9 Tenant key management centralized in the cloud with no administrative overhead on-premises

This centralized topology is the default topology; it is appropriate for companies that don't want to have an extra layer of administrative tasks to perform on-premises. However, some companies with more restrictive security policies or compliance requirements, or companies that are more skeptical about allowing the cloud provider to manage their protection key, might want to evaluate the hybrid topology. In the hybrid topology, the company is responsible for generating the master key on-premises, securing the key, and performing the appropriate level of backup for this key. (These are administrative tasks that you don't have to deal with when you adopt the centralized topology.) After the key is generated on-premises, it needs to be securely transferred to the Microsoft HSM used by Azure RMS. The key can be transferred either in person by contacting Microsoft Customer Service and Support (CSS) or it can be transferred over the Internet. After this transference is performed, Azure RMS will use this key to protect company data. Figure 7-10 shows this topology.

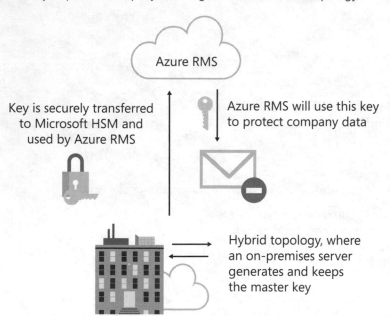

FIGURE 7-10 In the hybrid topology, the company is responsible for generating and maintaining the key

The adoption of this hybrid topology means that the company will bring its own key to be used by Azure RMS; this process is also known as Bring Your Own Key (BYOK). One key requirement to adopting BYOK is that the company must have access to a Thales HSM and have a local personal with enough knowledge to operate the Thales HSM[3]. Another factor that will impact the decision on which topology the company should use to adopt Azure RMS is the available operations for key lifecycle. Table 7-1 compares these two options.

TABLE 7-2 Comparison of key options

Key operation	Default option (managed by Microsoft)	BYOK (managed by the company)
Revoke your tenant key	No (automatic)	No (automatic)
Re-key your tenant key	Yes	Yes
Back up and recover your tenant key	No	Yes
Export your tenant key	Yes	No*
Respond to a breach	Yes	Yes
If you use BYOK, you cannot export your tenant key from Azure RMS. The copy in Azure RMS is non-recoverable		

> **TIP** For the complete list of steps to adopt BYOK, read the TechNet article at *http://technet.microsoft.com/en-us/library/dn440580.aspx#BKMK_ImplementBYOK*.

Azure RMS connector

Another option for companies that want to leverage the Azure RMS capabilities by integrating them with on-premises servers is the use of the Azure RMS connector. With this connector, IT administrators and users can easily protect their data both inside the organization and outside, without having to install additional infrastructure or establish trust relationships with other organizations. The Azure RMS connector supports the following on-premises servers: Exchange Server, SharePoint Server, and file servers that run Windows Server and use File Classification Infrastructure (FCI). To use this feature, you must have directory synchronization between your on-premises Active Directory and Azure Active Directory (see Chapter 4 for more details on how to perform this synchronization).

For fault-tolerance purposes, the Azure RMS connector should be installed in at least two computers located on-premises. Although it is not required to have a dedicated computer to install the Azure RMS connector, you should not install the Azure RMS connector in your resource servers, such as Exchange Server, SharePoint Server, or a File Server with FCI. You should also plan to use HTTPS to secure the communication from on-premises servers using the Azure RMS connector with Azure RMS in the cloud. Ensure that each server that has the connector installed has a valid server authentication certificate and that they trust the root

---

[3] For more information about how to use an on-premises (local) Thales nShield® HSM to generate crypto-graphic key for Azure RMS, visit *http://aka.ms/AzureRMSHSM*.

Certificate Authority (CA) that issued the certificate. In this setup, each server that has the RMS connector insta lled will have a certificate that contains the name that you will use for the connector (for example, *rmsconnector.blueyonderairlines.com*) and this name should be defined in the DNS. Figure 7-11 shows this topology.

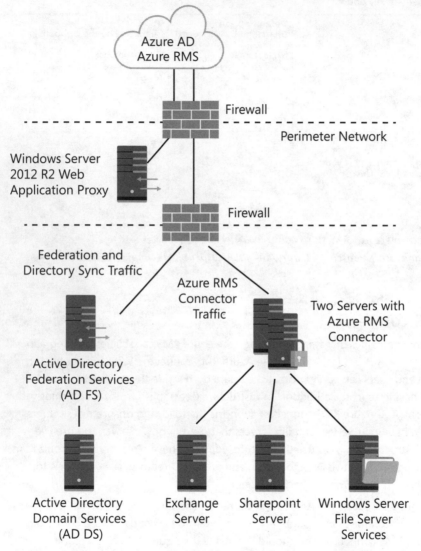

FIGURE 7-11 Components that are involved in an infrastructure that supports the Azure RMS connector

In the example shown in Figure 7-11, the Web Application Proxy has an HTTPS publishing rule for AD FS federation connectivity with Azure AD. The use of Web Application Proxy in this scenario is not a requirement as long as you have another solution to securely publish your on-premises applications. The diagram also shows two servers with Azure RMS connector for fault-tolerant and load-balancing purposes. It is important to mention that once you have both servers configured, you can use any IP-based load balancer to enable the Azure RMS connector clients (Exchange Server, SharePoint, and File Server) to see this Azure RMS connector as a single entity. If you choose to use the Network Load Balancing (NLB) feature available in Windows Server, you need to configure the Affinity to None and the Distribution Method to Equal.

> **IMPORTANT**   The RMS connector must be configured to use an account that has Microsoft RMS Tenant Global Administrator or Microsoft RMS Connector Administrator account privileges.

> **MORE INFO**   For more information about publishing AD FS via Web Application Proxy, read the TechNet article at *http://technet.microsoft.com/en-us/library/dn528859.aspx*. For more information on how to deploy Windows Network Load Balancing, read the TechNet article at *http://technet.microsoft.com/library/cc754833(v=WS.10).aspx*.

Monitoring access to resources

When dealing with data access and protection as a pillar for enterprise mobility adoption, it is important not only to keep control over the data, but also to understand how this data is being consumed by the users. Azure RMS enables IT administrators to monitor Azure RMS usage, which includes requests coming from users and Azure RMS-related tasks performed by IT administrators or users that were delegated to operate the Azure RMS service. By closely monitoring these aspects of the service, it will be easier to identify potential abuse of the protection service, track data access for forensics purposes, or just perform data analysis to understand patterns.

To use Azure RMS logging, you need to create an Azure Storage account using your Azure subscription and use Windows PowerShell for Azure RMS to configure this storage. (For information on installing Windows PowerShell for Azure RMS, go to *http://technet.microsoft.com/en-us/library/jj585012.aspx*.) Azure RMS will write the logs in this Azure Storage account that you created by using a series of blobs. Each blob will contain one or more log records that will be using W3C extended log format. You can use the Azure Administrative Portal to see these logs or you can download these logs using Windows PowerShell for your on-premises servers. Figure 7-12 shows a diagram of this distribution.

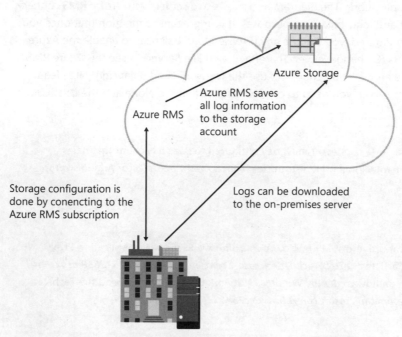

Azure Storage

Azure RMS saves all log information to the storage account

Azure RMS

Storage configuration is done by conencting to the Azure RMS subscription

Logs can be downloaded to the on-premises server

FIGURE 7-12 Key components for enabling and reviewing Azure RMS logs

> **TIP** You can use the Get-AadrmUsageLog cmdlet to download Azure RMS logs to your computer. By using this cmdlet, you can download each blob as a file and save it in the location that you specify in the command.

Figure 7-13 shows an example of how this log format appears in the management portal.

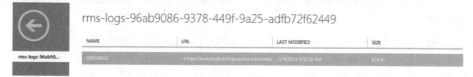

rms-logs-96ab9086-9378-449f-9a25-adfb72f62449

NAME	URL	LAST MODIFIED	SIZE
000000001	https://blueyorderairlines.blob.core.windov...	11/9/2014 3:51:42 PM	620 B

rms-logs-96ab90...

FIGURE 7-13 Example of the Azure RMS log format

If you decide to download the log files form Azure Storage to your on-premises server, ensure that the destination server is in a secure location, the storage that these logs will be saved is encrypted, and that only authorized users will have access to it. Logging can reveal many of the user's behaviors and therefore should not be open to everyone in the organization. If necessary, you can delegate access to your RMS logs by sharing your storage account name and access key. There are many scenarios in which the IT administrator might want to share access to these logs with other administrative users or with a developer who is using this storage as part of his app development. Although it might sound risky to share your account name and access key, this is a safe procedure because this storage is dedicated to your RMS logs, which means that even though other users will have access to the key, they can't use this key to access any other storage in the management portal.

## Chapter 8

Implementing data protection

In Chapter 7, you learned about data access and protection, including the importance of leveraging built-in capabilities in the Windows operating system to help you protect data and how Azure Rights Management Services (RMS) can be used to provide another level of security for the data.

In this chapter, you take on the role of the senior enterprise administrator for the Blue Yonder Airlines IT department and implement data access and protection as the third phase of their EMS implementation plan as described at the end of Chapter 2. You will be responsible for implementing security controls to mitigate potential data leakage and also ensure that Blue Yonder Airlines' data is classified according to the level of confidentiality.

Scenario description

As the senior enterprise administrator for Blue Yonder Airlines, you are responsible for planning, designing, and implementing the company's EMS solution. You know that data access and protection is a fundamental part of the strategy to enable a mobile workforce, so you will start here.

The majority of company's critical data is located on-premises; however, when users start consuming this data from mobile devices, the security of this data will be at a greater risk. Since the integration between the existing on-premises Windows Server Active Directory and Microsoft Azure AD is already complete, you can leverage a single identity as part of the process to authenticate and authorize users' access to data.

Implementation goals

The goals for the third and final phase of the EMS implementation plan for Blue Yonder Airlines are:

- To protect and classify data
- To mitigate issues related to data leakage on mobile devices

Solution diagram

To meet the EMS implementation goals for the first phase of the project, you need to implement the solution shown in Figure 8-1.

Each quadrant of the solution represents an area with specific security risks and concerns. The diagram shows how users accessing applications and services from their personal devices are authenticated by on-premises Active Directory Federated Services (AD FS) and Active Directory Domain Services (AD DS) while keeping the data secure across all locations. The four quadrants of the solution diagram are:

- **Corporate network** The corporate network, *corp.blueyonderairlines.com*, is where the on-premises core infrastructure resides. Many files that will be accessed by remote users are located in the on-premises Windows Server 2012 R2 File Server.

- **Perimeter network** The perimeter network (sometimes called a demilitarized zone or DMZ) is where the Web Application Proxy was installed in Chapter 4.

- **Users and devices** This part of the solution diagram represents the Blue Yonder Airlines employees and the devices they use on a regular basis—both company-owned and employee-owned. Notice that the goal here is to keep data protected regardless of who owns the device.

- **Cloud services and applications** This section represents the cloud services and Software-as-a-Service (SaaS) applications that Blue Yonder Airlines' employees access using their devices. Company data must be protected when in the cloud.

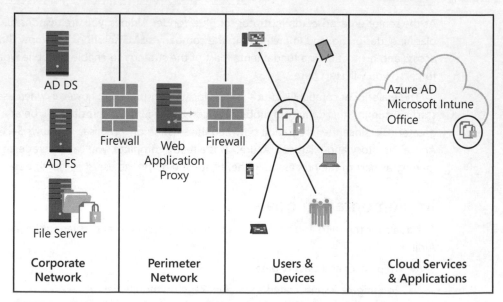

FIGURE 8-1 Data access and protection diagram for the enterprise mobility solution

Planning and designing the solution

Next, you want to build on the solution diagram by identifying the individual technologies and configuration requirements needed implement the mobility strategy. You need to completely understand the information in this section to plan and prepare for the configuration steps necessary to successfully complete this phase of the project.

This section is meant to provide you with additional details about the components and considerations while implementing the data access and protection pillar from EMS. The next section will guide you through the actual implementation steps and show you what each component looks like in more detail.

Leveraging Azure RMS

As already discussed in Chapter 7, Azure RMS is a cloud-based service that provides data protection capabilities for Azure resources as well as all Microsoft cloud services such as Microsoft Intune and Office 365. You will not use EMS's full potential until you leverage Azure RMS capabilities to protect company data. The design process for Azure RMS starts with identifying which topology is the best fit for your business requirements. The topology that best fits the requirements for Blue Yonder Airlines is the centralized-in-the-cloud topology, where Microsoft manages the Master Key. Blue Yonder Airlines is also using Office 365, therefore the mail system is also located in the cloud and the integration with Azure RMS is automatically done once you enable this feature in Azure AD.

> **MORE INFO** All other major design considerations for Azure RMS, including requirements, are presented in Chapter 7.

Preparing the environment

After identifying the topology, the next step is to prepare the environment that will support Azure RMS. IT administrators, or anyone else who is responsible for managing Azure RMS, should install the Azure Rights Management Administration Tool on their computers. This tool installs the Windows PowerShell module for Azure Rights Management, which you will need to manually perform some tasks and to automate others.

> **MORE INFO** You can download this tool from *http://go.microsoft.com/fwlink/?LinkId=257721*.

After installing this tool, you should be able to manage Azure RMS from the workstation where the tool was installed. However, before managing Azure RMS, you must activate Azure RMS using the Azure Management Portal.

1. On the Azure Management Portal, sign in using your Azure account.

2. On the left pane, click Active Directory to open the Active Directory page.

3. Click the Rights Management tab, select the directory you want to manage for Rights Management, click Activate, and then confirm your action. When Azure RMS is activated, your directory is listed as Active, as shown in Figure 8-2.

FIGURE 8-2 Azure RMS status when it is activated

> **TIP** At this point, you can go back to the computer where the Azure Rights Management Administration Tool was installed, open Windows as an administrator, and type **Import-module –name aadrm** to import the Azure RMS modules and **Get-Command -Module aadrm** to visualize the commands available. To test connectivity with Azure RMS from Windows PowerShell, use the command **Connect-AadrmService**. For more information about how this command works, visit *http://msdn.microsoft.com/library/azure/dn629415.aspx*.

After the activation is performed, you can click in the directory name under NAME and the Azure RMS options will appear, as shown in Figure 8-3.

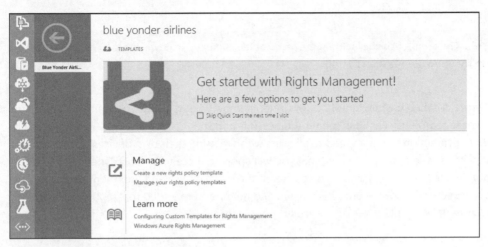

FIGURE 8-3 Azure RMS configuration options

These options allow you to create new templates that can be consumed by applications, such as email (Outlook) or documents (Microsoft Office Word).

Implementing the solution

Azure RMS plays an important role in meeting the requirements for data protection. To implement the requirements for Blue Yonder Airlines, you must complete the following two sets of configurations:

- Configure a set of templates with settings that are more restrictive than the default template settings to protect docu ments and emails.
- Configure file classification to integrate the on-premises file server with the Azure RMS service.

Configuring Azure RMS templates

To protect company data that is located in files, Azure RMS can enforce policies by using rights policy templates that have predefined restrictions, such as user rights and content expiration. The advantage of using templates is that they provide a way for users to apply permissions to protected content. By default, the following two templates are available within Azure RMS:

- **Confidential View Only**   This template is applicable for all users within the organization; it gives users with access to the data permission to view the content only.

- **Confidential** This template allows all users to perform the following tasks: View Content, Save File, Edit Content, View Assigned Rights, Allow Macros, Forward, Reply, and Reply All.

> **TIP** The template name includes the name of the company that was specified when signing up for an Azure AD subscription.

Before creating custom templates, you should know what it is that you want to accomplish with these templates. For Blue Yonder Airlines, it is important to have a more restrictive policy for data protection that is applied to all users who are using their own devices. You can do this by creating a custom template that you will apply to these users only. One approach is to obtain a list of all users who have registered their own device and add them to a group in Active Directory. Once the group is created and members are added to it, you can enforce the Azure RMS template to that particular group only.

> **IMPORTANT** After creating the custom template, users will not see it immediately. You need to publish the template to make it visible to users.

Creating a custom template

Since you have an EMS subscription, the tool that you will use to create a custom template is the Azure Management Portal. Sign in to the Azure Management Portal with global administrator credentials and complete the following steps to successfully create and publish your custom template:

1. In the left pane, click Active Directory.

2. On the Active Directory page, click Rights Management.

3. Select the directory to manage for Rights Management.

4. From the Get Started With Rights Management Quick Start page, click Create A New Rights Policy Template.

5. In the Add A New Rights Policy Template dialog box, choose the language in which you will type the template name and description that users will see. Type a unique Name and a Description, and then click the Complete (check mark) button, as shown in Figure 8-4.

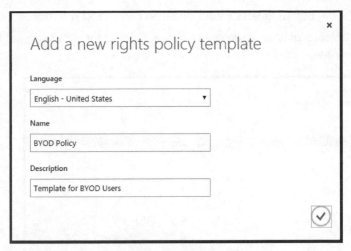

FIGURE 8-4 Adding a name to the new custom template

6. On the Get Started With Rights Management Quick Start page, click Manage Your Rights Policy Templates.

7. On this new page, the new template that you just created appears with a status of Archived. Click the template to edit it.

8. From the Your Template Has Been Added Quick Start page, click Get Started, Configure Rights For Users And Groups.

9. On the Select Users And Groups page, click the group that you want to add and it is added to the Selected pane on the right, as shown in Figure 8-5.

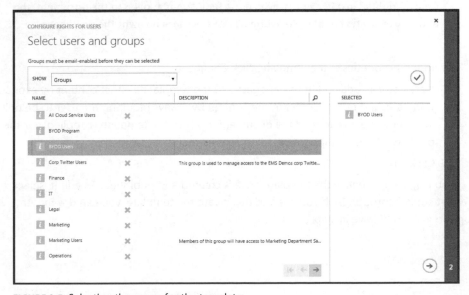

FIGURE 8-5 Selecting the group for the template

10. Click the Next (arrow) button, select Custom, and then click the Next button.

11. On the Assign Custom Rights page shown in Figure 8-6, select the rights you want to assign to the template.

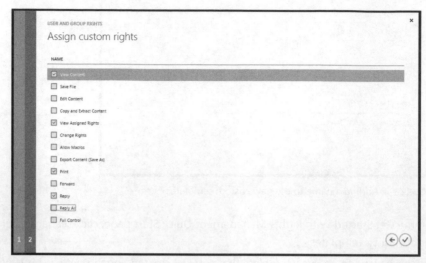

FIGURE 8-6 Selecting the rights for the custom template

12. Click the Complete (check mark) button.

> **IMPORTANT** After you assign rights to the template, a page opens that states the following important information: "The author of a protected document always has Full Control rights." In other words, even if the template is applied to the document, the author will always be able to perform all tasks because he owns the document.

13. In the proprieties of the template, click Configure.

14. Here you can add additional languages to the template, restrict content by expiration date, and restrict access to the content by always requiring the user to be online in order to be able to read the document in which the template is applied. For the purpose of this example, leave all options as-is and click Publish.

15. Click Save.

You can always change the template once is created and published. To edit it, select it and repeat steps 7 through 14. If you need to deactivate the template, you can use the Archive option instead of Save in Step 15.

Applying a custom template to a document

After the template is created and published, it is ready to be used. Different client apps will have different steps to implement the template. Microsoft Office 2013 has native support for Azure RMS; however, the first time you use the document protection feature in Microsoft Office 2013, there is an initial step that must be done, which is to connect to the Rights Management Server.

Using Microsoft Word 2013 as the sample application, follow these steps to perform this initial setup:

1. Open your document and select the File tab to access the Info page.

2. Click the Protect Document button, point to Restrict Access, and click Connect To Rights Management Servers And Get Templates, as shown in Figure 8-7.

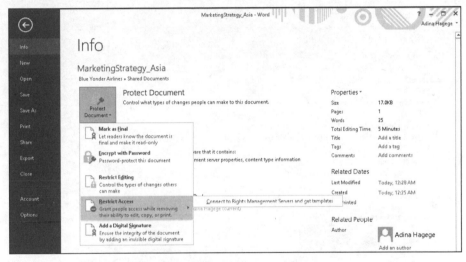

FIGURE 8-7 Initial connection with the Rights Management Server

A message will appear stating that templates are being retrieved from the server; when this action finishes, the Microsoft Word interface is displayed again.

These steps are necessary only in the beginning. After your profile is configured and the application knows that it needs to obtain the templates from the server, you will not need to perform these steps again. The templates that appear in the Microsoft Office 2013 list of templates are automatically refreshed every 7 days.

If you need to change the behavior on the client side to receive a template immediately, change the registry value TemplateUpdateFrequency under HKEY_CURRENT_USER\Software\Classes\Local Settings\Software\Microsoft\MSIPC to specify the frequency in days. Remember that you must be careful when making changes in the registry. If you use the Registry Editor incorrectly, you can cause serious problems that might require you to reinstall the operating system.

> **IMPORTANT** Use the Registry Editor at you own risk. Microsoft policy states that they cannot guarantee that you can solve problems that result from using the Registry Editor incorrectly.

After the template is published, you can use the same Protect Document button and you will see the template that you created, as shown in Figure 8-8.

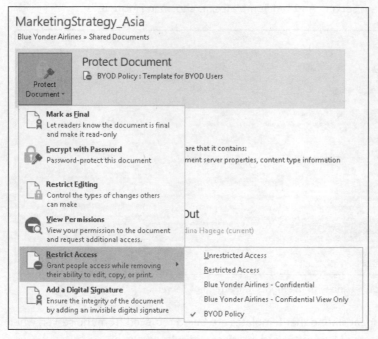

FIGURE 8-8 A template correctly published and now available for the user

> **IMPORTANT** Although this example uses Microsoft Word 2013, the RMS templates will be available for consumption from all supported platforms. For a list of other supported applications, see the article at *http://technet.microsoft.com/library/dn339006.aspx*.

This document is saved in the Blue Yonder Airlines SharePoint shared documents folder. When a member of the BYOD Users group tries to open this document, she will receive a warning similar to the warning shown in Figure 8-9.

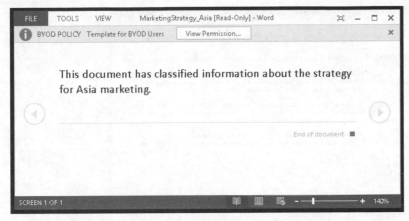

FIGURE 8-9 A user that has restrictive access to the shared document

With this implementation you fulfill the first requirement for data protection, which is to configure a set of templates with restrictive settings to protect documents and emails. In the next section, you will work to fulfill the second requirement, which is to configure file classification to integrate the on-premises file server with the Azure RMS service.

Azure RMS connector

To fulfill the second data protection requirement established by Blue Yonder Airlines, it is necessary to install the Azure RMS connector on a dedicated server located on-premises. As mentioned in Chapter 7, the Azure RMS connector is required for scenarios in which you need to integrate Azure RMS with on-premises workloads, such as the File Server. For fault-tolerance purposes, it is recommended that you install the Azure RMS connector on at least two servers.

The File Server should be a domain member; it should have the File Server role installed and the File Server Resource Manager (FSRM) feature enabled. To install the Azure RMS connector on this server, you must have administrative privileges on the local machine. Although you can use HTTP for the RMS connector, consider obtaining a certificate for the RMS connector. The subject for this certificate must be resolvable by your internal DNS Server and, if you are using a load balancer between two Azure RMS connector servers, the name should resolve for the load-balance alias.

The server on which you are installing the Azure RMS connector requires Internet Information Services (IIS). If IIS is not already available, the installation process should add it as part of the setup.

Log on using a domain account with administrative privileges on the member server where the Azure RMS connector will be installed, download the Azure RMS connector from *http://go.microsoft.com/fwlink/?LinkId=314106* onto this server, and complete the following steps:

1. Run the executable file RMSConnectorSetup to open the Microsoft Rights Management Connector Setup Wizard shown in Figure 8-10.

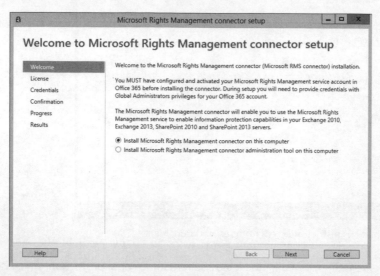

FIGURE 8-10 The first page of the Microsoft Rights Management Connector Setup Wizard

2. The default option is to install the connector on this computer. Leave this option selected (as shown in Figure 8-10) and click Next.

3. On the End-User License Agreement page, read the license terms, select I Accept The Terms In This License Agreement, and click Next.

4. On the Microsoft RMS Administrator Credentials page, type the credentials for an account that has administrator privileges on the Microsoft RMS tenant (Microsoft RMS Tenant Global Administrator) or an account in Azure Active Directory (Azure AD) that has been granted rights to install and administer the RMS connector for the organization (Microsoft RMS Connector Administrator). Click Next.

5. On the Ready To Install Microsoft Rights Management Connector page, click Install. Notice that the Install button has the symbol that represents a potential prompt for consent. If the user that you are installing this tool for does not have local administrative privileges, you will be prompted for credentials.

    The Installing Microsoft Rights Management Connector page shows a progress bar with the elements that are getting installed. When it finishes running, you will see the Installation Of Microsoft Rights Management Connector Completed page, as shown in Figure 8-11.

FIGURE 8-11 Microsoft Azure RMS connector successfully installed

6. Assuming that your file server is already installed and ready to obtain RMS Templates from Azure, leave the Launch Connector Administration Console To Authorize Servers check box selected and click Finish. The Microsoft Rights Management Connector Administration Tool opens, as shown in Figure 8-12.

FIGURE 8-12 The initial screen for the Microsoft Azure RMS Connector Administrator Tool

7. Click the Add button, and in the Allow A Server To Utilize The Connector page, select FCI Server from the Role drop-down list box, as shown in Figure 8-13.

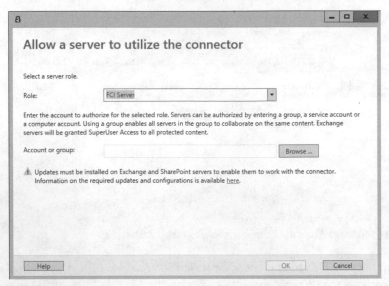

FIGURE 8-13 Selecting the role and the servers that will be allowed to use this connector

8. Click Browse next to Account Or Group and select the File Server that will be authorized to use this connector. Next, click OK twice and then click Close.

   At this point the Azure RMS Connector is installed and configured on one server. For redundancy purposes, you should repeat this procedure and install the Azure RMS Connector on a second server.

9. To test your installation was successful, connect to the server using URL *http://<connectoraddress>/_wmcs/certification/servercertification.asmx* from the server where the connector is installed. After accessing this address, you should see a webpage similar to that shown in Figure 8-14.

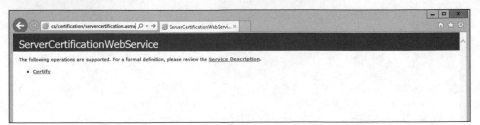

FIGURE 8-14 The Azure RMS connector webpage that can be used to validate the successful installation of the tool

Configuring File Server to use Azure RMS

To be able to leverage the Azure RMS templates for data protection, the File Server that will be configured to use Azure RMS must have the FSRM feature installed on it. Make sure you enable this feature because it is not enabled by default when you install the File Server role on a server.

After confirming that the FSRM feature is installed, download the GenConnectorConfig.ps1 tool from *http://go.microsoft.com/fwlink/?LinkId=314106* on the file server. After downloading this tool, log on to this File Server using a domain account with administrative privileges in the local computer and complete the following steps:

1. Open Windows PowerShell with elevated privileges.

2. Type the command **GenConnectorConfig.ps1 –SetFCI2012 –ConnectorUri http://FQDNfortheAzureRMSConnector**.

3. If you receive the following warning message, press A.

   ```
   File C:\temp\GenConnectorConfig.ps1 is published by CN=Microsoft Corporation,
   OU=MOPR, O=Microsoft Corporation, L=Redmond, S=Washington, C=US and is not trusted
   on your system. Only run scripts from trusted publishers. [V] Never run   [D] Do
   not run   [R] Run once   [A] Always run   [?] Help (default is "D"): A
   ```

4. The prompt should be available after pressing A and you can validate the inclusion of the URL by looking at the value in the registry key HKEY_LOCAL_MACHINE\SOFTWARE\Microsoft\MSDRM\ServiceLocation\EnterprisePublishing. It should match the URL that you typed in Step 2.

5. Open Services.msc and restart the FSRM service.

Configuring file classification

Now that the File Server is configured to use Azure RMS as its main repository for templates, you can create file management tasks that can leverage templates created in Azure RMS. There are many approaches that you can use to perform this task; this section covers the approach of using file classification. For example, all users who are storing files in the Financial folder located on this server will automatically have their documents classified as confidential. This will be accomplished by automatically applying a specific template from Azure RMS that has the required restrictions.

Before you can begin, you must complete the following prerequisite steps on the File Server.

- On your on-premises Active Directory, you need to:
  1. Enable the required attribute (in this case, Department) that will be used when evaluating the Dynamic Access Control (DAC) condition.

2. Configure the properties that will be downloaded by file servers and used to classify files. DAC rules will compare user attribute values with resource properties. You will enable the existing Department property to match the department claim.

3. Create a central access rule to describe which conditions must be met for file access to be granted. In this specific rule, you will require the Department attribute.

4. Create a central access policy to enforce the rule.

5. Publish the central policy using Group Policy.

- On the File Server, you need to use FSRM to:

   1. Validate that a classification policy was created as the result of the publication of the central policy using Group Policy.

   2. Create a classification rule that uses the Department property to classify files that contain the string "confidential" in the file content and are saved in the C:\Financial folder.

IMPORTANT To read more about how to configure DAC in Windows Server 2012 R2, visit *http://technet.microsoft.com/en-us/library/hh846167.aspx*. For more information about FSRM, visit *http://technet.microsoft.com/en-us/library/hh831701.aspx*.

After completing the prerequisite steps, use the FSRM to configure a file management task that will apply the Azure RMS template. Log on to the file server as a user with administrative privileges and complete the following steps:

1. Open Server Manager and click Tools, File Server Resource Manager.

2. In the File Resource Manager tool, click the File Management Tasks node in the left pane.

3. Right-click in the File Management Tasks node and click Create File Management Task.

4. On the General tab, type the name of this task (for this example, Financial).

5. Click the Scope tab, select User Files, click the Add button, and select the folder that you want to manage with this task. For this example, the folder is C:\Financial.

6. On the Action tab, under the Type drop-down list, select RMS Encryption. The result should be the list of templates created in Azure RMS, as shown in Figure 8-15.

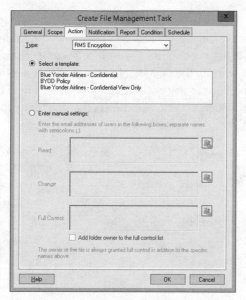

FIGURE 8-15 Templates retrieved from Microsoft Azure RMS

7. Select the template. For this example, the selected template is Blue Yonder Airlines – Confidential.

8. On the Schedule tab, select the days of the week on which this task will run. For this example, it will run all days, including Saturday and Sunday. Click OK to finish.

You can wait for the schedule to take effect or you can right-click the task in the main section of File Resource Manager and choose the Run File Management Task Now option. In the lower pane, you will see a summary of the task and also the current status, as shown in Figure 8-16.

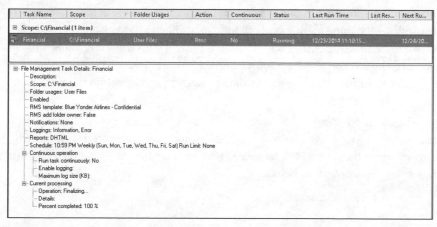

FIGURE 8-16 Summary of the file management task and processing status

Validating client access

The infrastructure is now ready to automatically classify any new files created in this folder. When a user saves a file in this folder, she will not need to use the Protect Document capability in Microsoft Office 2013 to manually classify the document. Instead, the file server automatically applies the RMS template conditions to any new documents. When a user tries to open a file that was saved in the Financial folder, a message indicates that the template was already applied, as shown in Figure 8-17.

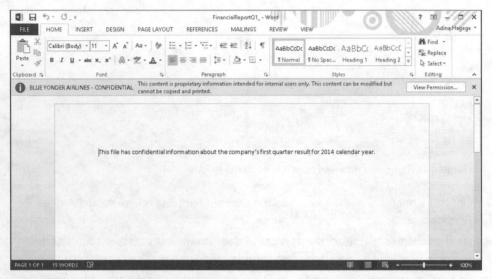

FIGURE 8-17 An Azure RMS template automatically applied to a file that contains the required string

Integrating Azure RMS with Work Folders

You are making significant progress in the implementation goals that were established. Next, you need to address the last implementation goal for data protection, which covers data leakage. As was explained in Chapter 7, it is important to protect data while it is at rest in the user's device because this can also be a source of data leakage. You will now leverage Windows Server 2012 R2 capabilities to enhance data protection and integrate them with Azure RMS.

In Windows Server 2012 R2, Work Folders allow users to store files on the File Server, making it possible to work with these files offline while keeping them protected. This feature can also take advantage of the Azure RMS templates that were created to protect documents. Figure 8-18 shows how this integration works.

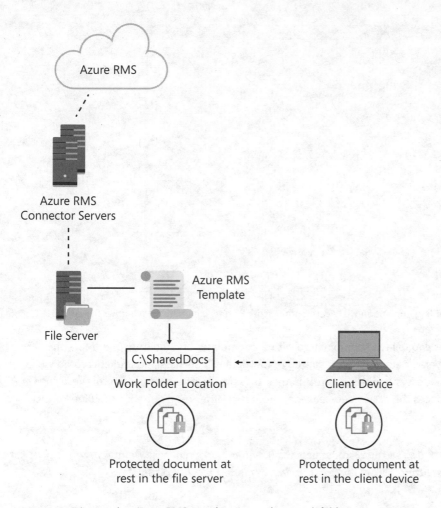

Azure RMS

Azure RMS
Connector Servers

File Server

Azure RMS
Template

C:\SharedDocs

Work Folder Location

Client Device

Protected document at
rest in the file server

Protected document at
rest in the client device

FIGURE 8-18 Leveraging Azure RMS templates to apply to work folders

From the Azure RMS and File Server perspective, the steps are similar to the ones that were previously explained in the file classification section in this chapter. To enhance data protection for Work Folders, you should ensure that encryption is required. You can do that while enabling Work Folders in the File Server using the New Sync Share Wizard, as shown in Figure 8-19.

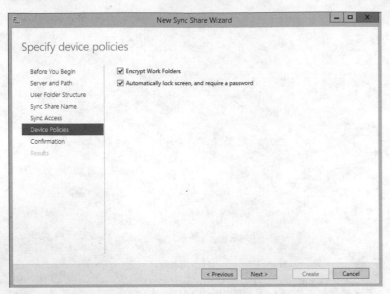

FIGURE 8-19 Enabling encryption while configuring Work Folders capability in Windows Server 2012 R2

By using this capability in combination with the templates created in Azure RMS, you enhance the overall data protection strategy. Now data will be classified and encrypted while at rest in the file server and while at rest in the user's device. The combination of these capabilities also reduces the risk of data leakage, which is another requirement from Blue Yonder Airlines.

> **IMPORTANT** To read more about how to configure Work Folders in Windows Server 2012 R2, visit *http://technet.microsoft.com/en-us/library/dn528861.aspx*.

## Chapter 9

Monitoring BYOD and company-owned devices

The next part of your strategy for a mobile workforce is to enable IT to stay in control while also enabling users to be productive. From the implementation perspective, you already learned how to do that, but now you need to keep the system working properly and, if necessary, be able to identify why it is not working.

In this chapter, you take on the role of the senior enterprise administrator for Blue Yonder Airlines IT to leverage EMS capabilities for monitoring resources and responding to security incidents.

Continuous monitoring and incident response

You need to ensure that IT can control your organization's data both on-premises and on remote devices. You will need to implement continuous monitoring of users' activities and understand how devices are being used to consume data. The IT department and the Security department should work together to identify any suspicious activities and react to them based on an established plan, which is part of the incident response plan.

Monitoring users and devices can also assist IT in identifying trends and proactively mitigating potential issues. For example, if an IT administrator repeatedly sees alerts regarding multiple failure attempts to log on from one user's credential during a particular time of day, the administrator might suspect that someone other than the user is trying to log on with the user's credentials. The administrator might investigate further to identify what is happening and why.

Before you start monitoring users and devices, you should formulate a monitoring plan. Begin by answering some important questions to help you develop the plan. Here are some sample questions that you can use to start your monitoring plan:

- What assets are you trying to protect?
- What are the threats against them?
- What vulnerabilities might these assets have?
- What's the likelihood that those threats will materialize?
- What do you consider an authentication anomaly in your environment?

These sample questions will assist you to build the foundation for your monitoring strategy and from there you can create more granular questions to target specific areas relevant to your organization. In conjunction with monitoring, you also need to understand how incident response takes place in the overall security strategy. Figure 9-1 shows three security phases—prevention, detection, and reaction—and how they fit into a monitoring plan.

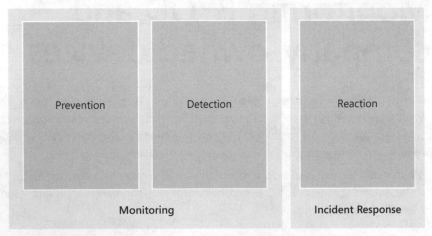

Prevention	Detection	Reaction
Monitoring		Incident Response

FIGURE 9-1   The different security phases and where each activity fits into them

Figure 9-1 is an example of one way to fit the security phases into monitoring and incident response. Organizations with custom requirements might decide to break down these phases or expand on them. Large organizations might already have an incident response plan in place, in which case they need to identify how the plan will be affected when they are adopting enterprise mobility. The basic concept is that monitoring is a task that has direct impact in preventing and detecting security-related issues. Incident response is about how the organization will react to an incident when a security-related issue occurs.

Don't overlook the learning process as a part of your incident response plan. Always ask what you learned from an incident and how can you prevent it from happening again. This learning will enable IT to enhance their monitoring scope to add attributes that were not previously considered because the company didn't know about that potential threat. As you can see, this is an ongoing process and that's why it is important to keep things aligned between proactive (monitoring) tasks and reactive (incident response) tasks.

Creating an incident response plan

This section addresses some of the key aspects of an incident response plan and what you need to consider to incorporate enterprise mobility into your plan. This is a huge topic and you can find long papers, such as *Responding to IT Security Incidents*[1], that explain about all elements of an incident response plan.

---

[1]   You can read this paper at *http://technet.microsoft.com/en-us/library/cc700825.aspx*.

All employees of the organization must know how to react if they think a security breach might have occurred. If an employee is travelling and he believes his system is compromised, he needs to know whom he should contact first and what actions he must take. If a procedure is not well established or the employee is not aware of how to report an incident, he will try to troubleshoot it himself, which can be harmful in different levels. First, he might not have the technical expertise to resolve the issue; second, he might be removing evidence that could be used to identify the root cause of the problem.

A good incident response plan should, at a minimum, include procedures for the following items:

- Evaluate the current state of the system by verifying the:
  - Extent of the infection
  - Type of data at risk
  - Source or target of the attack
  - Resources that were compromised
  - Resources that are suspected to be compromised
  - Impact on infrastructure
  - Cost of recovery
- Establish the first course of action in a detailed response plan
- Isolate and contain the threat
- Track and identify the attacker
- Analyze and respond to the incident
- Alert others according to the response strategy
- Begin system remediation and clean-up
- Detail the de-escalation process
- Detail the post-incident review process

Several of these procedures might have ramifications. For example, the post-incident review process should include details on what needs to be documented, the lessons that were learned, and how to enhance the overall security to prevent this type of incident from happening again. If the incident isn't preventable, at least add countermeasures that can reduce the likelihood that will happen again.

Leveraging EMS to monitor resources

Throughout this book you have seen how the three cloud services that are part of EMS can assist you in enabling users to be more productive with their devices while keeping IT in control of company data

Because EMS is composed of three cloud services, is very important for the IT administrator to understand the monitoring capabilities of *each* cloud service. With this knowledge, the IT administrator will understand which cloud service she needs to use to obtain specific types of information about the user or device. Figure 9-2 is a pictorial summary of this relationship.

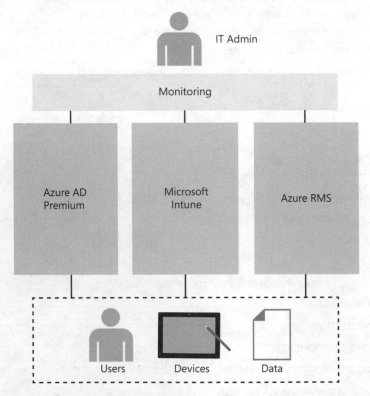

FIGURE 9-2 The IT admin should leverage the reporting and monitoring capabilities of all three cloud services to monitor users, devices, and data

Azure AD monitoring capabilities

As you learned in Chapter 3, you can use access and usage reports to gain visibility into the activity and security of your organization's Azure AD environment. You can use the information from these reports to determine where possible security risks might exist and then plan how to mitigate those risks.

> **MORE INFO** While all Azure AD reports are useful, the anomalous activity reports are the primary focus of this chapter. You can learn more about all of the available Azure AD access and usage reports on MSDN at *http://msdn.microsoft.com/library/azure/dn283934.aspx*.

As a tenant administrator, you should review all Azure AD reports on a regular basis to ensure that you are aware of any possible security threats. You will need to investigate and take action to mitigate any potential risks that you discover. After you implement EMS for your organization, you will have access to several Azure AD Premium reports (in addition to the standard reports) that are useful in detecting anomalous behaviors, including those shown in Figure 9-3.

⊿ PREMIUM REPORTS	
Sign ins from IP addresses with suspicious activity	May indicate a successful sign in after a sustained intrusion attempt.
Sign ins from possibly infected devices	May indicate an attempt to sign in from possibly infected devices.
Irregular sign in activity	May indicate events anomalous to users' sign in patterns.
Users with anomalous sign in activity	Indicates users whose accounts may have been compromised.
Password reset activity	Provides a detailed view of password resets that occur in your organization.
Password reset registration activity	Provides a detailed view of password reset registrations that occur in your organization.
Groups activity	Provides an activity log to all group related activity in your directory
Application usage	Provides a usage summary for all SaaS applications integrated with your directory.

FIGURE 9-3   The Azure AD Premium reports made available as part of EMS

As shown in Figure 9-3, the premium reports are:

- **Sign Ins From IP addresses With Suspicious Activity**   When multiple sign-in attempts fail over a short period of time or other suspicious activity occurs from the same IP address, it could indicate that someone other than the trusted user is trying to gain access to the account or company resources. You should review this report on a regular basis to discover all sign-in attempts originating from suspicious IP addresses.

- **Sign Ins From Possibly Infected Devices**   This report should be reviewed to ensure that your users are not signing in on devices that might be compromised with malware. If a user's device is assigned an IP address that was recently used to contact a malware server, the device and sign-in information will be available in this report.

- **Irregular Sign In Activity**   This is a powerful report, based on machine learning, which will alert you to abnormal sign-in activities. There are several ways that the service could determine that a sign-in is irregular, such as multiple sign-in locations in a very short period of time. The algorithm used to determine this behavior will classify the sign-in as either irregular or suspicious. If an event is marked as suspicious, you should definitely investigate the issue because it has a higher chance of being a security breach than an irregular event.

- **Users With Anomalous Sign In Activity** This report gives you a single view of all user accounts for which anomalous sign-in activity has been identified through any anomalous reporting method. This report includes details about the user and other relevant information about the event.

- **Password Reset Activity** This report provides you with an overview of the password reset activity that is occurring within your organization.

- **Password Reset Registration Activity** This report provides you with an overview of the password reset registrations that are occurring within your organization.

- **Groups Activity** This report provides you with information about the activities occurring within Azure AD groups. This includes changes to group memberships as well as other basic group activity.

- **Application Usage** This report provides you with an overview of how Software-as-a-Service (SaaS) applications that are integrated with your Azure AD directory are being used. It displays the application name, the number of unique users accessing that application, and how many total sign-ins have occurred during the time period you specify for the report (the last 30 days, the last 7 days, or the previous 24 hours).

Besides simply viewing the data when a report is generated, you can sort the data by any of the resulting report columns or use the search box capabilities built into the report to search for specific data. If you need to save a copy of the report, you can use the Download option provided at the bottom of the report page to Open or Save a .zip file containing a copy of the report data in .csv format, as shown in Figure 9-4.

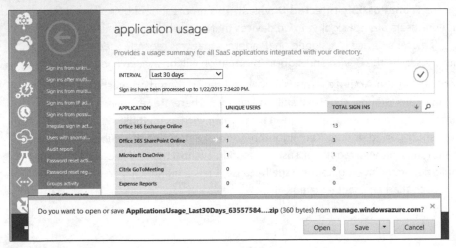

FIGURE 9-4 The Open or Save options for Azure AD reports

Microsoft Intune monitoring capabilities

Microsoft Intune provides alerts and reports that can be used to monitor the service to provide a high-level view of device health and inform you of issues that should be addressed. Just as you should review Azure AD reports on a regular basis, you should also respond to Microsoft Intune alerts in a timely manner and regularly review the reports available to you.

Microsoft Intune alerts

Microsoft Intune alert types can be thought of as pre-configured rules that generate an alert that is displayed in the main Admin Console dashboard, as shown in Figure 9-5.

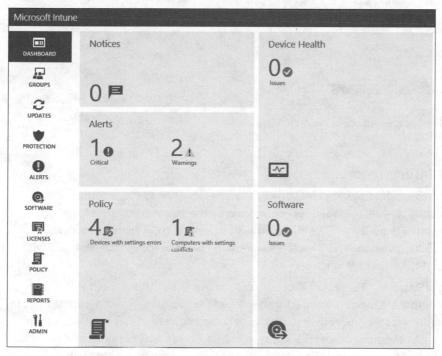

FIGURE 9-5   The Alerts section of the Admin Console dashboard

You can configure alert types in the Admin Console by browsing to Admin, Alerts and Notifications, Alert Types. From there, you can change default alert settings and enable or disable alerts based on your preferences and needs. This is also where you define email notification recipients who will receive emails generated by the Microsoft Intune service when an alert is triggered. While there, you can also define when those emails are sent for the various alerts by customizing the notification rules to meet your notification requirements.

After you configure alert types, you can view detailed alert information for any alerts generated by the service in the Alerts workspace of the Admin Console. The Alerts Overview dashboard displays a summary of active alerts that you can review with a quick glance. You can display and sort active alerts by date, category (endpoint protection, monitoring, notices, policy, remote assistance, system, or updates), or severity (critical, warning, or informational) and also pick a sort option to choose to place either the newest or oldest alerts on top of the list. To dive deeper into a specific alert, click the alert notification itself or drill-down into the various alert categories for more information, as shown in Figure 9-6.

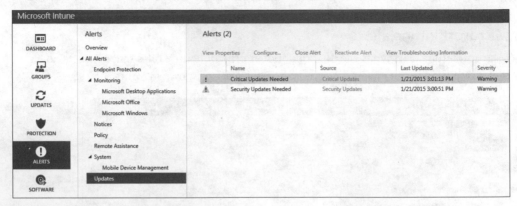

FIGURE 9-6 The Alerts workspace of the Admin Console

Microsoft Intune reports

The reporting capabilities provided by Microsoft Intune allow you to stay informed about activities occurring in your managed service and can be used to help you plan for future hardware or software purchases. The following built-in reports are available to provide information about inventoried hardware, software, and license usage in your Mobile Device Management (MDM) environment:

- **Update Reports**   This report allows you to discover information about software updates that are pending, needed, installed, or failed on managed computers. You can also easily filter the report data to display only the information you need, such as the update classification, Microsoft Security Response Center (MSRC) rating, and whether or not you have defined the update as not applicable or should be installed.

- **Detected Software Reports**   This report displays software that has been detected on computers managed by the Microsoft Intune service. This report allows you to further refine reported results by device group, software publisher, or software category.

- **Computer Inventory Reports**   This report displays hardware information that has been detected on computers managed by the Microsoft Intune service. Customizable criteria for this report include device group, manufacturers, chassis type, operating system, model, or even physical hardware information such as available disk space, physical memory, or CPU speed.

- **Mobile Device Inventory Reports**   Similar to the computer inventory report, this report displays information collected about mobile devices being managed by your Microsoft Intune service instance. Results for this report can be scoped to a particular device group, operating system, and also whether the device has been jailbroken or rooted.

- **License Purchase Reports**   When you add license agreement information (either Microsoft Volume License Agreements or other license agreements) to your Microsoft Intune service from the Licenses workspace in the Admin Console, the agreement information is displayed in these reports.

- **License Installation Reports**   This report enables you to see at a glance how many software licenses you have purchased for licensed software and how many managed computers have that software installed. This report can be useful in ensuring that you are using software legally in your environment, but the service will not stop detected software from running or being installed if you run out of software licenses.

- **Terms And Conditions Reports**   Using this report, you can view which users have accepted your custom terms and conditions. In addition to the user name, you also see which version of the terms and conditions was agreed to and on what date the action occurred.

- **Noncompliance Apps Reports**   If you have created and deployed configuration policies for Android or iOS devices, this report can be used to view app compliance status for users and their devices. You can filter this report to show app installations from either the compliant or noncompliant apps list that you have previously defined as part of the configuration policy.

- **Certificate Compliance Reports**   This report displays information about certificates that have been issued to users and devices from the Network Device Enrollment Service (NDES). NDES is one of the role services of the Active Directory Certificate Services (AD CS) and it implements the Simple Certificate Enrollment Protocol (SCEP) to provide communication between network devices and a Registration Authority (RA)[2].

- **Device History Reports**   Historical information about when a device is retired, wiped, or deleted is displayed in this report based on the date range that you specify. With this report, not only do you have a historical record of the action taken, but also information about the device name, owner, state, and who initiated the action.

---

[2]   You can learn more about how SCEP is used for certificate enrollment at *http://tools.ietf.org/html/draft-nourse-scep-18*.

When a Microsoft Intune report is generated based on the criteria that you have selected, you can easily view it in a new browser window. You can sort the data by any column and all of the report data is searchable via the search box in the top-right corner of the data display area, as shown in Figure 9-7.

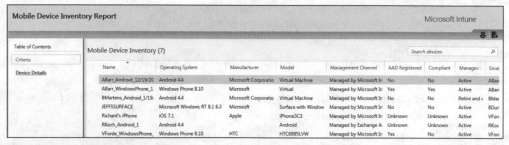

FIGURE 9-7 The Mobile Device Inventory Report as displayed in a web browser.

Additionally, in the top-right corner, each report provides you with options to print the data or export it as a .csv or .html file (see Figure 9-8).

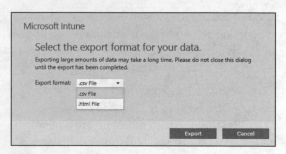

FIGURE 9-8 The Microsoft Intune report export dialog box

While each of the built-in reports allows you to customize the data displayed by selecting the criteria most important to you, it can be time consuming to do this on a regular basis. Another option you have is to save a customized report so that you can quickly access the necessary information without needing to re-customize the built-in report every time. To do this, just customize the report so that it displays the information that you want to see and then use the Save As option in the top-right corner of the reports workspace to save the custom report. The list of built-in report names on the left side of the workspace will not change, but the next time you select the built-in report that you have customized, you will be able to quickly access the customized report from the Load drop-down menu on the right side, as shown in Figure 9-9.

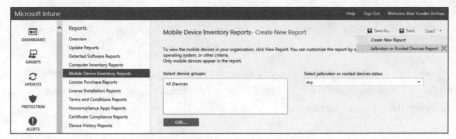

FIGURE 9-9 Loading a customized Microsoft Intune report

Microsoft Azure RMS monitoring capabilities

As you learned in Chapter 7, Azure RMS enables IT Administrators to monitor Azure RMS usage, which includes requests coming from users and Azure RMS-related tasks performed by IT Administrators or users who were de legated to operate the Azure RMS service. The storage that has the Azure RMS log will show minimal information if you just look at the Dashboard, as shown in Figure 9-10.

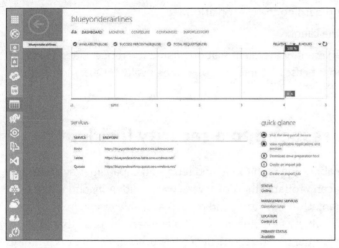

FIGURE 9-10 Information about the storage that has the azure RMS logs

There is not much information to extract from the dashboard, but if you click Containers, you can access the logs and download them. When you download a log, it opens in a new tab in your browser and shows more details, as shown in Figure 9-11.

FIGURE 9-11 Azure RMS logs

In this log, you can identify activities such as a client requesting a license for a specific piece of content, a client requesting a certificate from a Windows-based computer, and request queries for the URLs to certify and acquire licenses. This log file contains the following fields:

- **Date**   The date in which the request was made. This date is in UTC format.
- **Time**   The time in which the request was made. This time is in UTC 24 hour format.
- **Row-id**   The unique GUID for the log.
- **Request-type**   The RMS API that was used in the request.
- **User-id**   The username that represents the user that started the request.
- **Result**   The type of result, which shows if the request was done successfully or not.
- **Correlation-id**   The common GUID used between RMS client and server.
- **Content-id**   The GUID for the protected content.
- **C-info**   The information regarding the client platform.
- **C-ip**   The IP address of the client.

With this information, you can identify the client that originated the request, and if you are working on an incident response case, this information can be useful for a compromised account.

Leveraging EMS to respond to a security incident

Now that you understand more about the monitoring and reporting capabilities available to you with EMS technologies, you can probably think of several ways to identify and mitigate security issues in your environment. Using the tools and reports available to you in a holistic way gives you greater control and ability to rapidly respond to any security issue that might arise as you work to keep control of the organization's data while users are either on-premises or remote.

For the remainder of this chapter, you will again assume the role of the senior enterprise administrator for Blue Yonder Airlines and take the necessary steps to identify threats and take proactive actions to mitigate potential security issues using EMS technologies.

Scenario

As the senior enterprise administrator for Blue Yonder Airlines you are responsible for the overall monitoring and security strategy for the company. In addition to regular monitoring of the service and your users' actions, the security strategy also outlines a clear incident response strategy built upon the capabilities provided by your EMS implementation for the airline.

Prevention

The first monitoring component of the security strategy you have developed for Blue Yonder Airlines is prevention. You have taken great effort during the planning and implementation phases of your EMS rollout to harden the security of your environment as much as possible while still providing the flexibility for your end users to easily use their own devices at work.

Beginning with on-premises Active Directory integration with Azure AD, you enabled hybrid identity and single source control of directory objects anywhere. In the Blue Yonder Airlines Azure AD, you have also required that all users register before accessing the Azure Access Panel applications and settings and you have also forced users to define multiple authentication methods for password resets and multi-factor authentication (MFA) applications. Requiring all users to enroll their devices in Microsoft Intune Mobile Device Management in order to access Microsoft Exchange email enables you to help protect access to company resources and control several aspects of the devices themselves without infringing on employee privacy. Finally, you have implemented Azure RMS as a final defense to protect company data. These proactive steps have set you up to both safeguard against security issues and to quickly respond to any security incidents.

Detection

Many security incidents go unnoticed in today's enterprise environments. It is your job as the senior enterprise administrator for Blue Yonder Airlines to ensure that you and your IT management team are preforming due diligence and monitoring the services used by your users on a regular basis to identify any possible anomalies. To accomplish this task, you regularly review the Azure AD reports available to you as well as monitor the Microsoft Intune service alerts and reports.

While reviewing Azure AD reports, you notice anomalous activity associated with one of Blue Yonder Airlines employees named Ben Martens. According to the Users With Anomalous Sign In Activity report shown in Figure 9-12, Ben Martens' attempts to sign in failed multiple times before he finally successfully gained access to company resources. In addition to the several failed sign-in attempts, the report indicates that this account has been logged into from several geo-distant locations within a very short period of time. Each of these issues will need to be further investigated to determine what is going on with this account.

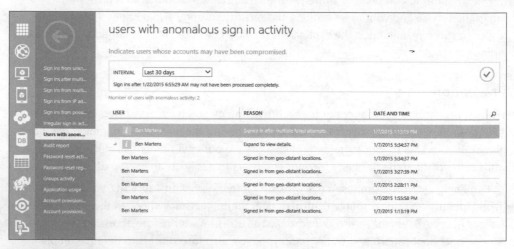

FIGURE 9-12 The Users With Anomalous Sign In Activity report

The first issue discovered is that the user, Ben Martens, has tried unsuccessfully to log in multiple times before finally gaining access to company resources at myapps.microsoft.com. This kind of behavior could indicate a brute force password attack using this user's credentials. To investigate further, you review the Sign Ins After Multiple Failures report shown in Figure 9-13 and discover that this account had over 100 failed sign-in attempts before finally signing in successfully. By looking more closely at the report data, the date and time stamps of each failed log in attempt reveal they were all made in less than 15 minutes before a successful sign-in took place. These sign-in attempts also originated from an IP address that you do not recognize and from a city not associated with any Blue Yonder Airlines operations.

FIGURE 9-13 The Sign Ins After Multiple Failures report

Continuing your investigation into this possible security breach, you review the Sign Ins From Multiple Geographies report and discover even more unsettling information about this possible security breach. This report shows that the user account was used to successfully authenticate into the Blue Yonder Airlines cloud services infrastructure several times on the same day from several different geographic locations from all over the world, as shown in Figure 9-14. Adding to your suspicions, according to the work info recorded in this user's account properties, Ben Martens is located in Franklin, Massachusetts, and does not travel to Europe on a regular basis.

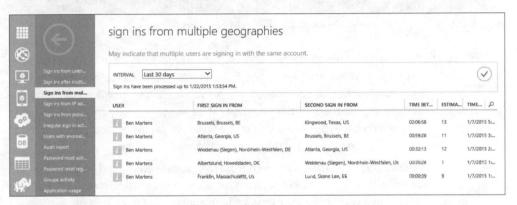

FIGURE 9-14 The Sign Ins From Multiple Geographies report

Reaction

After identifying this incident through monitoring, and evaluating it as a viable threat to company resources, the next step is to respond to the security breach and take action to isolate and contain the threat.

You immediately enable MFA on Ben Martens' account in Azure AD, as shown in Figure 9-15, which will require him to provide both his password and a security code via text message or phone call before he can access company resources.

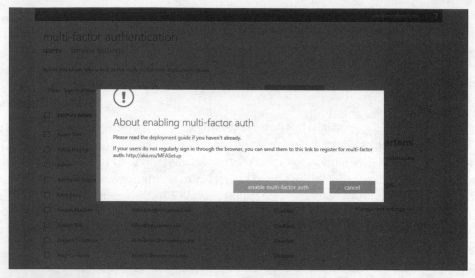

FIGURE 9-15 Enabling MFA for a potentially compromised user account

Next, you use Microsoft Intune to identify Ben Martens' primary device and send a remote lock command to ensure that the device is locked from unauthorized access. You also try to call his office phone number, but he does not answer, so you leave a voice mail requesting him to call you as soon as possible with the warning that he will soon lose access to company resources if he does not contact you by the end of the business day. As an additional method of reaching out to him, you send an email outlying the same expected behavior.

At the end of the day, you still have not heard from him, so you are forced to block his access to Blue Yonder Airlines cloud resources from his account properties in Azure AD, as shown in Figure 9-16. Then you notify your boss and the appropriate people in the security and legal departments about the possible security breach.

FIGURE 9-16 Disabling a user's access to cloud services from his Azure AD account properties

The next day, a helpdesk phone call is escalated to you. The call is from Ben Martens, who is complaining about having to verify his account by text messages and explaining that he is encountering errors when trying to sign in. He needs to access his work documents stored in his team's SharePoint site and he needs to access his Exchange web mail from myapps.microsoft.com from his home. He is very upset and blaming you for his lost productivity and threatening to call your boss if you do not make his issue your top priority.

Thinking through your incident response procedures, you calmly reply to him that his issue is definitely your top priority. Because he can't access his email, at least you now understand why he never responded to email; also, he's been working from home, so that's why he never returned your phone call yesterday. When you ask him why he's using the Azure Access Panel instead of the Exchange profile and Microsoft OneDrive app on his Android tablet device he normally uses, he becomes silent for a moment and then sheepishly admits that his tablet was stolen recently, so he has been using his wife's laptop to access company resources from home while he has been sick. He assures you that he was going to report the tablet stolen when he got back to the office. You probe further to determine whether his account password could have been compromised and he says there is no way it could have been compromised because, while the password that he had written on a note with his user name in his tablet case was a password that he had used in the past, it was one character different than his current password. There is no way anyone would ever figure that one out, right?

Suddenly, the entire situation becomes clear to you. What you now believe is that when Ben Martens' tablet was stolen, his password was easily hacked by whoever found the note in the case. Judging by the number of failed sign-in attempts on his account, it must not have taken long for the attackers to gain access to the account and then share the account information with others all over the globe. You transfer Ben to someone in the security department who will take care of the post-incident and review process and then you continue the final remediation and clean up steps available to you.

Due to the lax security precautions with his password, you are confident that his tablet was secured by a weak PIN and you plan to wipe the device as soon as possible (rather than just reset the passcode) to prevent any further data leakage or unauthorized access. After reading the Terms And Conditions report to verify that Ben Martens accepted the latest terms and conditions for using his personal device at work, you return to his account properties in the Microsoft Intune Admin Console to use the Retire/Wipe option to force a factory reset on his Android tablet, as shown in Figure 9-17.

> **TIP** Before you wipe a user's personal device, you should always review the Terms And Conditions report to ensure the user has accepted the terms and conditions for using his personal device at work and that these terms and conditions include the possibility of administrators wiping their device in situations such as this.

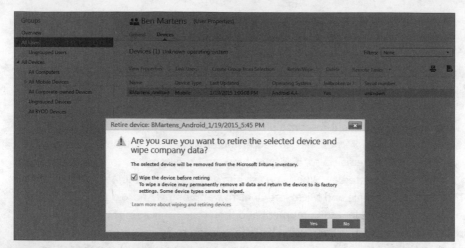

FIGURE 9-17 Wiping a possibly compromised Android table device

You immediately see a notification in the console that tells you the device is now in the process of retiring and, once the wipe process is complete, the device's status will no longer appear in the Admin Console. You make a note to check the Device History report later in the day to ensure the remote wipe process completed successfully and, finally, you then take an early lunch after sending a meeting invite to your boss to discuss your next raise.

## Chapter 10

Troubleshooting Enterprise Mobility Suite

Ideally, your implementation will work smoothly and require minimum intervention other than the normal monitoring processes that were explained in the previous chapter. However, when deploying new technologies in your environment, it is common to face challenges that might require additional steps in order to work properly. This is where support comes in to perform proper troubleshooting of the problem. Because Enterprise Mobility Suite (EMS) is composed of three cloud services, there are different techniques that should be leveraged to properly isolate any issue and fix it.

In this chapter, you will learn key aspects of how to properly troubleshoot an issue regardless of the problem and then you will learn more details about the supportability capabilities of each cloud service available via EMS.

Troubleshooting methodology

If your car won't start, you immediately believe something is wrong. You try again and, based on the sound that it makes, you create a hypothesis about what is causing the problem. You might try one more time and listen to the sound it makes to either be more confident regarding the accuracy of your hypothesis or create more than one hypothesis as to the cause of the problem. You try to implement steps to fix what you thought was the problem, but the car still will not start and continues to make the same sound. At this point, while you still have the problem, you have eliminated one possible cause of the problem.

Observing the behavior, taking notes of what you observe, formulating a hypothesis, and implementing steps that should address the root cause of the issue if the hypothesis is correct: this is what is known as troubleshooting. Several times experienced IT professionals fail to follow the correct troubleshooting sequence and fail to isolate the problem. However, a good troubleshooter understands the logic and how the process should flow. The process is always the same. Even if you don't have deep product knowledge, you will still be able to identify and isolate the issue. You might not resolve the problem if you don't have enough expertise, but you can complete the most difficult part of the process.

One of the biggest mistakes you can make during the troubleshooting process is to improperly scope the problem. For example, a user calls the helpdesk and says that his

Internet is down. The first-level helpdesk technician needs to ask a broad range of questions to start troubleshooting the problem. When Internet access is lost, there can be several causes. What should the technician ask?

- Does the issue happen only when accessing this website or does it happen when accessing all websites?
- Which website are you trying to access?
- When did this issue first occur?
- Did you make any configuration changes in the system?
- Have you tried to access this website from another computer?
- Does anyone else use this computer?

These sample questions will help you isolate the problem, eliminate hypotheses, and create new ones. For example, if the answer to the first question is "No," the response should be "Try to access bing.com." If it doesn't work, you don't even need to ask the second question and will move on to the third question. You might end the initial call with narrower scope, such as "The user, Adina, is having issues trying to access our organization's website when he is using his computer; however, it works fine from another computer in the same network. No changes were done in the system according to the user and no one else has access to this computer." This is a much better scope because here you have a specific behavior that you will troubleshoot further without wasting time trying things that are not relevant for this scenario.

Another important aspect of troubleshooting is to start with the basics; do not ignore simple mistakes. Sometimes experienced IT professionals might be caught trying to resolve issues on the application layer while the problem is actually in the network layer. A classic example of this is trying to resolve a connectivity issue using a browser by leveraging advanced debugging browser tools while the problem is that the host didn't have a route to reach the destination. What about using the tracert tool before you start using advanced tools? This approach will save you time and make your troubleshooting much more effective because you are eliminating phases without jumping into an abstraction mode that will only lead you to create a false hypothesis of what could be the root cause of the problem.

This troubleshooting methodology can be applied in any situation and any product. It will evolve as you gain more experience with the platform and the product itself, which will allow you to think quickly and come up with a more accurate hypothesis that could be tested right away. The following list is a suggested troubleshooting flow that can assist you through this process:

1. **Conduct an initial assessment** Get a complete explanation of the problem, the symptoms that the user is experiencing, whether the user changed any setting in the system, when the issue started to happen, whether this capability ever worked, and whether the issue always happens or if it is random. If it is random, try to obtain more information regarding patterns; for example, ask questions like:

   - Does it happen at a particular time of the day (morning, afternoon, or night)?

- Are you doing any specific activity when you notice this issue happens (for example, while running a specific program)?

2. **Create initial documentation**   Documenting all details that were obtained in the initial assessment is the key to successful troubleshooting. The documentation not only enables you to follow up and see what symptoms were, but it also helps you to create a knowledge base. By saving the documentation for all troubleshooting cases that you deal with, you will build a solid database that can be used for research and quick fixes based on similar issues.

3. **Elaborate on one or more hypothesis**   After reviewing the initial documentation and all the data that was collected, elaborate on the potential hypothesis for the problem. Make sure you prioritize each hypothesis based on the likelihood each issue might be the problem. At this point you want to avoid trying several things at the same time; you want to avoid potential confusion while building your conclusion of what the real issue was.

4. **Collect data**   The next step is to obtain data while the issue is happening. Configuring tools that you use to collect data while reproducing the issue can help to either confirm that you are headed in the right direction (your hypothesis is correct) or that you should look to different issues in the system.

5. **Analyze the data**   Data analysis is a very important part of the troubleshooting process. Make sure you use the right tools to analyze the data. This will help not only to better interpret the output but also to make the process more agile. It is very important to emphasize that sometimes data analysis can take a long time. The amount of time depends on the amount of data that you have to analyze.

6. **Create a plan of action**   Next, create an action plan and try to fix the issue. You should also evaluate how this action plan might affect productivity, asking yourself questions such as "What are the collaterals that might happen if I execute this?" At this point, you might not know the answer because you might not know the variants of the environment. Good communication is crucial. Ask questions about the environment and exchange ideas with your user regarding the potential consequences of the plan. The plan of action should be a step-by-step approach to help you track what you have done and make it possible for you to reverse what you've done, if necessary. It also helps other people from your organization to understand what has been done. The plan of action should be documented in the case notes.

7. **Implement the plan of action**   The implementation should be carefully done to avoid disruption of the system (unless the system is already completely down). Make sure you understand the ramifications of the plan. For example, if during the implementation you need to install a hotfix, validate that the hotfix will restart the target machine. It is also very important to have a backup plan in case an implementation step causes other problems in the production environment.

8. **Validate the results**   After implementing the action plan, you must validate whether the issue was resolved. At this point, you need to try to reproduce the same scenario

that was occurring when the issue was detected. It is important to recognize that in some cases this is not possible. For example, random issues might not appear in normal circumstances, which means that you must leave the system in a monitoring state and wait to see if the issue happens again.

9. **Create closure documentation**   After the problem is fixed, you need to document the final considerations regarding the implementation, behaviors observed, and the final results. It is important to write a conclusion for the case, stating the technical aspect of the problem and determining the root cause of the issue.

Knowing where to find information

If you are going to support a product, it is important to understand where that particular product stores information for troubleshooting purposes. Most Microsoft products store information in the Event Viewer, which is a good place to start to obtain information about the particular problem you are experiencing. However, in some situations, you might need a more detailed log that can give you more explanation about what's happening at a particular point in time.

For a mobile workforce, knowing where the logs are located for each device platform can be challenging. Each platform might have its own requirements for increasing the logging information to verbose and also the location where the log is stored. Always refer to the vendor's documentation for more information about support and operations.

Using troubleshooting tools

Troubleshooting tools can vary according to the platform and the troubleshooting scenario. Some platforms might offer a specific set of tools to collect data and another set of tools to automate the analysis. However, there are some scenarios in which generic tools can be used to obtain more information about the issue. For example, for network-related issues, you can use Network Monitor while reproducing the issue between the client device and the service (or service). If the traffic is encrypted, you can use Fiddler to assist you with obtaining and analyzing the data.

> **NOTE**   You can download Fiddler at *http://msdn.microsoft.com/en-us/library/windows/desktop/ff966510%28v=vs.85%29.aspx*.

Ensure that you have a variety of tools available and that each platform that you have to support includes instructions on how to use those tools not only to obtain the data but also to interpret the logs that those tools will generate. Another strategy that can help when validating the results generated by those tools is to have a testing environment that can reproduce problems, obtain data, and analyze that data. You can use emulators for mobile devices and basically reproduce your production environment in a virtual lab.

Troubleshooting EMS cloud services

When troubleshooting EMS, you should leverage the same methodology that was explained earlier in this chapter. In addition, consider the fact that you will be dealing with three cloud services, which means that the troubleshooting steps can get broader if you don't have the correct scope of the issue. For example, if the helpdesk receives a call from a user saying that he can't launch an app that he just installed via the company portal, this can be a very broad scope and more than one cloud service might be involved in this issue. Can it be the authentication? What about the permissions in the app? Can it be a local problem on that particular device? As you learned earlier in this chapter, these are questions that are part of the initial assessment and must be documented as part of determining the right scope for the problem.

In the sections that follow, you will learn more about troubleshooting best practices and techniques for each cloud service that is part of EMS.

Troubleshooting Azure AD Premium

For the most part, Azure AD Premium "just works," but there are some areas that might be a little more difficult to configure or troubleshoot than others. This section describes a few common problems you might encounter while trying to use Azure AD Premium features and how to quickly resolve them.

As stated earlier in this book, everything begins with identity synchronization; if you cannot get that working seamlessly, it can impact your entire EMS deployment. You don't need to worry about a maximum number of objects being synchronized into Azure AD with an EMS subscription, but to really get started, you will definitely need to have some user account information synchronized from your on-premises environment to the cloud.

The Azure AD Connect Wizard makes configuring AD FS and Single Sign-On (SSO) a breeze with its simple guided experience, but one thing that it does require when working its magic is Windows Remote Management (WinRM) functionality—the Microsoft implementation of the WS-Management Protocol that is firewall friendly because it operates over http and https. So when running the Azure AD Connect Wizard to implement directory synchronization, the remote server that you choose to install the Web Application Proxy server on must have WinRM enabled. If that server does not have WinRM enabled or configured, you will most likely get an error in the wizard that looks something like what is displayed in Figure 10-1.

FIGURE 10-1 WinRM connection error while installing the Web Application Proxy using the Azure AD Connect Wizard

Fortunately, this issue is very easy to resolve by simply enabling the WS-Management protocol on the server you want to use as the Web Application Proxy. To accomplish this, you need only to open a command prompt with administrator permissions and use the winrm quickconfig command to set up the default configuration for remote management. If all goes well, you will see something like Figure 10-2 and the wizard should be able to continue.

After successfully configuring identity synchronization and Active Directory Federation Services (AD FS), you will, of course, want to check to be sure everything is working properly. In most cases, everything will probably function just fine after using the Azure AD Connect Wizard, but if something is misconfigured or some other issue causes an interruption in identity authentication at a later date, you can quickly troubleshoot the issue using the Microsoft Connectivity Analyzer tool. This tool—which most Microsoft Exchange and Microsoft Office administrators are already familiar with—will help you to identify several problems related to your service—including SSO issues. This web-based tool is available at *https://testconnectivity. microsoft.com/*. From there, select the Client tab and then install and run the Microsoft Connectivity Analyzer Tool. Once it is installed and running, select the I Can't Set Up Federation With Office 365, Azure, Or Other Services That Use Azure Active Directory option to begin the testing process and then sign in with a federated user account that you have synchronized with Azure AD. If any issues are discovered, you will see a page similar to that which is shown Figure 10-3.

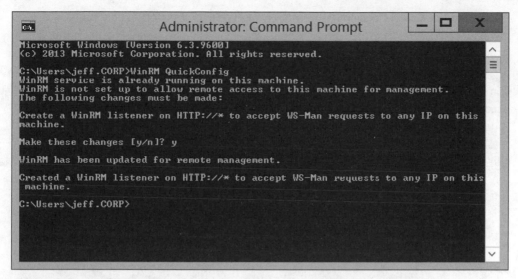

FIGURE 10-2 Using the winrm quickconfig command to set up the default configuration for remote server management

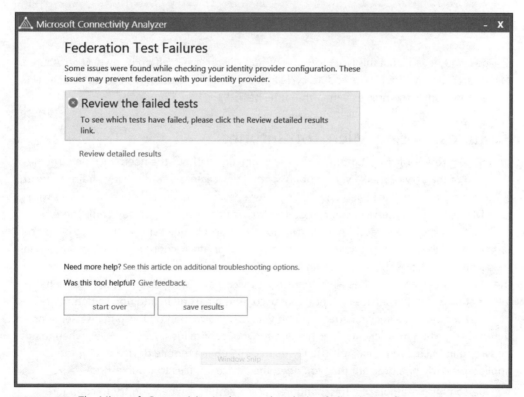

FIGURE 10-3 The Microsoft Connectivity Analyzer tool analyzing federation configuration

Clicking the Review Detailed Results option provides you with detailed information about any issues that were discovered that might prevent federation and identity authentication actions from being completed successfully.

Another behavior that you should be aware of is the delay in name resolution that can sometimes occur when reviewing Azure AD reports. For example, the first time that a user account is associated with one of the reports, the user name will be displayed as a seemingly random string of numbers, as shown in Figure 10-4.

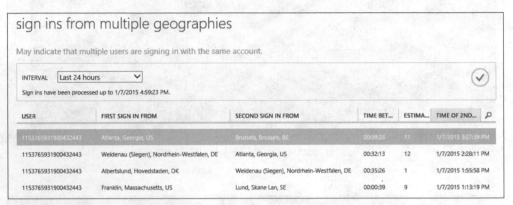

FIGURE 10-4 An unknown user account displayed in an Azure AD report

The good news is that this issue is transient and will resolve itself on its own. Most Azure AD reports run on a four-hour update cycle and any name resolution issues that you see like this should resolve themselves within that time period.

Troubleshooting Microsoft Intune

Just like Azure AD, Microsoft Intune will usually function without the need for much trouble-shooting of the service itself. Even troubleshooting device enrollment is fairly straightforward if you have configured the back-end infrastructure properly. To check for known issues with your Microsoft Intune service, you can go to *http://status.manage.microsoft.com*. There, you can see the current service status of all available Microsoft Intune service instances by geography. If you do not know what service instance your specific account is part of, you need only to log into the Microsoft Intune Admin Console and navigate to Admin, Learn About, and then select View Service Status. This opens the service status webpage with the additional information about the service instance your account is a part of. In addition to determining whether there is a known issue affecting you, the information on this page is useful for determining when maintenance is scheduled for your service instance. However, when things go wrong in Microsoft Intune, it is usually related to either a mobile device policy not being applied properly or a problem that you need the device log files to troubleshoot.

One common example of a misconfigured policy setting is when you try to configure company Microsoft Exchange email account settings via policy. If one of your users has already manually configured a Microsoft Exchange account to sync on his device using the default email app, Microsoft Intune policy will be unable to delete the original email profile information in order to install the one you specified in the email policy for the device. When that happens, the device becomes noncompliant with policy and, if you have conditional access configured, might end up with that device being totally blocked from accessing Microsoft Exchange email. Because Microsoft Intune policy cannot uninstall the preconfigured Microsoft Exchange profile your users, they will get a message like the one shown in Figure 10-5.

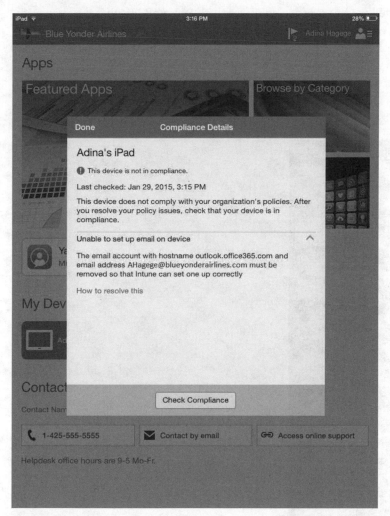

FIGURE 10-5 Compliance failure message when Microsoft Intune attempts to set up a Microsoft Exchange email profile that has already been manually configured

This issue is very easy for your users to resolve by simply going into their email settings, selecting the Exchange account they had previously configured, and then using the Delete Account option to remove the profile information from their devices. They can then go back into the Company Portal app to re-check for policy compliance. That will allow the Microsoft Exchange email policy to be configured in accordance with your corporate email configuration policy. When the email policy is applied, the company email profile will be installed and cannot be manually deleted. In fact, one way to verify that the email profile has been installed by policy is to check the email settings for your company Microsoft Exchange profile to verify that instead of seeing the Delete Account option, you see something similar to *These settings are installed by the profile 'Eas Profile – outlook.office365.comAHagege@blueyonderairlines.com.*"

Another policy-related aspect of managing devices with Microsoft Intune is the latency·in time from when a new mobile device management policy is deployed and when it is enforced on each type of device at their next normal policy polling interval (or when a new app is installed). To be sure that a user's device has the latest Microsoft Intune policy applied, you can trigger a manual policy sync by using the company portal app to check for compliance or sync the device with the Microsoft Intune service, as shown on a Windows Phone in Figure 10-6.

FIGURE 10-6   The check compliance option displayed in the Company Portal app on a Windows Phone

Of course, knowing that you have the most current policy applied doesn't help you much if you already know that a device is not compliant, but you don't know what to do about it. In cases like this, the best way to troubleshoot the issue is from the device policy settings shown in the Microsoft Intune Admin Console. There you can learn more about what you need to do to resolve an issue by reviewing the information available about the setting and recommended actions to take for each policy issue discovered, as shown in Figure 10-7.

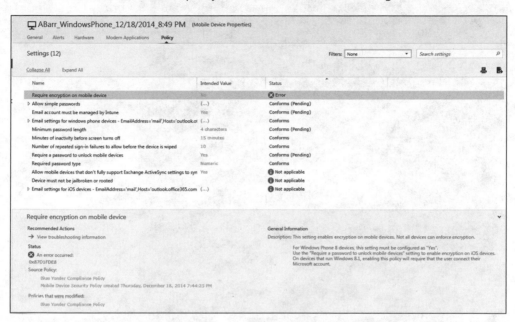

FIGURE 10-7 Information displayed for a device in the Microsoft Intune Admin Console about a policy error

The last line of defense for troubleshooting Microsoft Intune-managed mobile devices are the log files from the devices themselves. These are very simple for end users to access from the Company Portal app on all devices. Once obtained, all of the Company Portal apps already have built-in methods to share the log file results along with a screen shot to the administrator email address that you preconfigure in the Company Portal settings of the Microsoft Intune Admin Console. For Android and Windows devices, the log files can be generated and sent from simple menu options; iOS devices utilize a "shake and send" method of log file collection. With the Company Portal app open, you can just literally shake the iOS device to bring up the diagnostic information dialog on those devices, as shown in Figure 10-8.

FIGURE 10-8 The diagnostic information dialog box displayed when you use the "shake and send" functionality for iOS devices

When you select the option to email the logs, the administrator email address defined in the Microsoft Intune Admin Console for the Company Portal administrator contact will receive an email describing the issue. The body of the email will contain information about the device such as model and operating system. The email will also inform the administrator about any alerts that were captured describing the issue such as the Company Portal being temporarily unavailable. Attached to the email will be a screen shot of the device's screen when the logs were sent as well as a text log file named Company Portal-Log that contains detailed diagnostic information useful for further troubleshooting the issue.

Troubleshooting Azure Rights Management Services

As you learned in Chapter 8, setting up Azure Rights Management Services (RMS) is a pretty simple task; all of the configuration steps are done via the Azure Management Portal and once the configuration is completed, it will be up to the client to obtain that information. From that perspective, the cloud service itself usually is not the source of the troubleshooting unless the setup is wrong (for example, when a custom template is created and the permissions that you assigned to it are wrong). The problems that you might face that will require further troubleshooting are more related to the following areas:

- Client side issues
- Custom templates that are not available to the client
- Authentication-related issues on the client
- Client configuration issues
- Azure RMS connector

Depending on the source of the problem, the troubleshooting approach will be different, and the tools and the source of information will be different, too.

Troubleshooting the client side

One common misunderstanding about Azure RMS templates is that once you create or change them, they will be available to the client right away. There is an update interval for templates, which by default is 7 calendar days. In other words, the client will be retrieving updates from the server every 7 calendar days. Another misconception is that for that template to take effect, it needs to be updated on the client. But that is not necessarily true. For templates that were only modified, such as changes in the properties of the template, there is no need for that template to be refreshed on the user's device. The change will take effect when the user is consuming the protected content.

> **TIP** For more information about the default intervals and how to change it in Office 2013, visit *http://blogs.technet.com/b/rms/archive/2013/06/06/office-2013-ad-rms-client-2-x-and-template-distribution.aspx*.

By knowing the expected behavior, you avoid taking unnecessary troubleshooting steps for something that it is working as it should. However, if the client is unable to receive the template even after the interval expires, you should start the troubleshooting by validating that the client can perform the service discovery (discover.aadrm.com). To do that, ensure that the edge firewall is allowing access to the following URLs for HTTPS (TCP/port 443):

- Incoming and outgoing connections to *.aadrm.com
- Incoming and outgoing connections to *.cloudapp.net

To validate that this connection is working properly, use the following Windows PowerShell commands:

1. Open the Windows PowerShell command prompt with elevated privileges and type **Import-Module AADRM**.

2. Type **Connect-AadrmService –verbose** and wait for the authentication prompt. Make sure to use an account with global admin rights to perform this test.

3. Now that the connection is established, type **Get-AadrmConfiguration**. This command retrieves the Azure RMS configuration. Make note of the property LicensingIntranetDistributionPointUrl, because you will be using the value of this property in the next step.

4. Open Internet Explorer and type the value of \LicensingIntranetDistributionPointUrl and append the value **templatedistribution.asmx**. The entire URL should look similar to https://55a95263-388e-4c53-8c69-957705af910b.rms.na.aadrm.com/_wmcs/licensing/templatedistribution.asmx.

5. An authentication prompt might appear if you are not yet authenticated. Type the user's credential and verify that you can see the Template Distribution Web Service, similar to Figure 10-9.

FIGURE 10-9 The webpage that should appear when you type the distribution template URL

If your browser cannot reach this URL, the RMS client won't be able to either, which means that you need to troubleshoot network connectivity issues. Verify whether your client needs to have a proxy or whether your edge firewall is blocking this URL. If your browser is able to open this page, go back to Windows PowerShell and use the following sequence to obtain more information about the template that is failing to load:

1. List all templates available by using the command Get-AADRMTemplate. Take note of the TemplateId that represents the template that you are not able to see in the RMS client (for example, Microsoft Outlook). The output of this command should look similar to Figure 10-10.

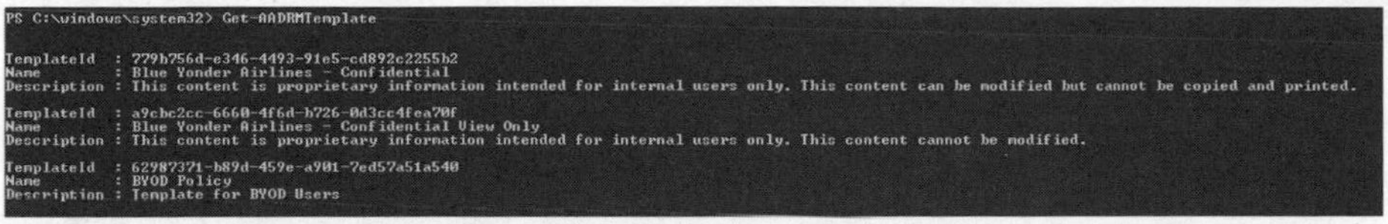

```
PS C:\windows\system32> Get-AADRMTemplate

TemplateId  : 779b756d-e346-4493-91e5-cd892c2255b2
Name        : Blue Yonder Airlines - Confidential
Description : This content is proprietary information intended for internal users only. This content can be modified but cannot be copied and printed.

TemplateId  : a9cbe2cc-6660-4f6d-b726-0d3cc4fea70f
Name        : Blue Yonder Airlines - Confidential View Only
Description : This content is proprietary information intended for internal users only. This content cannot be modified.

TemplateId  : 62987371-b89d-459e-a901-7ed57a51a540
Name        : BYOD Policy
Description : Template for BYOD Users
```

FIGURE 10-10 Windows PowerShell commands used to obtain more information about the templates

2. Type **Get-AADRMTemplateProperty -RightsDefinitions -*Templateid*** (using the Templateid from the previous step). In the value column of the output, ensure that the permissions are set up correctly.

One common mistake you'll find is that the user does not belong to the groups that are allowed to see the template. Make sure to confirm that before you proceed.

> **TIP** If you still experience problems on the client, more advanced troubleshooting will be necessary. For that, you can use the IRM Diagnostic Tool, which can be downloaded at *http://www.microsoft.com/en-us/download/details.aspx?id=43737*.

Troubleshooting the Azure RMS connector

In Chapter 8, you learned how to implement the Azure RMS connector and the prerequisites for installing this tool. It is recommended to have multiple servers with the Azure RMS connector installed for high-availability purposes.

Because the server that will have the Azure RMS connector is a member server, make sure that you have administrative rights on the local machine. Even if you log on as a domain administrator, if this account does not have administrative privileges on the server itself, you might receive the error shown in Figure 10-11 while installing the connector.

FIGURE 10-11 A not-so-intuitive error while installing the Azure RMS connector

This can be a very challenging problem to solve because the error message doesn't really explain why the problem occurred. In scenarios like this, you need to read the log file created by Azure RMS during the installation. This log is located in the user's %temp% folder, as shown in Figure 10-12.

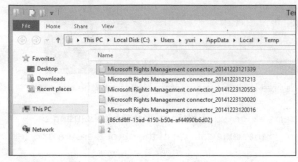

FIGURE 10-12 The location where the log files generated by the Azure RMS connector setup tool are stored

The best way to troubleshoot issues of this nature is to read all the way to the end of the file and trace it back to see where the error occurred. In this case, the error is highlighted in Figure 10-13.

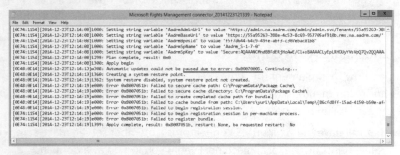

FIGURE 10-13 The content of the log file can be viewed using Notepad

By using the err tool, you will find out that the error 0x80070005 means access was denied, as shown in the output of the command:

```
err 0x80070005
# for hex 0x80070005 / decimal -2147024891 :
  COR_E_UNAUTHORIZEDACCESS                                corerror.h
# MessageText:
# Access is denied.
  DIERR_OTHERAPPHASPRIO                                   dinput.h
  DIERR_READONLY                                          dinput.h
  DIERR_HANDLEEXISTS                                      dinput.h
  DSERR_ACCESSDENIED                                      dsound.h
  ecAccessDenied                                          ec.h
  ecPropSecurityViolation                                 ec.h
  MAPI_E_NO_ACCESS                                        mapicode.h
  STIFRR_READONLY                                         stierr.h
  STIERR_NOTINITIALIZED                                   stierr.h
  E_ACCESSDENIED                                          winerror.h
# General access denied error
# 11 matches found for "0x80070005"
```

Another common mistake that can happen is to have the RMS connector on the same server as the role that you want to use to leverage Azure RMS (for example, the File Server role). If you want to have Azure RMS templates retrieved by the File Server, the Azure RMS connector should not be installed on the File Server itself. This type of mistake can cause the event shown in Figure 10-14 to happen when the Azure RMS connector tries to retrieve the templates in Windows Event Viewer.

FIGURE 10-14 Event details visible in the Application log in Event Viewer

Index

P

Q

R

X

Y

About the authors

 YURI DIOGENES is a Senior Content Developer on Microsoft's CSI Enterprise Mobility Team and has more than 20 years of experience in the IT field. He holds a Master of Science degree in Cybersecurity Intelligence and Forensics Investigation (Utica College) and has been working for Microsoft for the past nine years, including five years as a Senior Support Escalation Engineer on the CSS Forefront Edge Team. Yuri also holds an MBA and several industry certifications, including MCSE, MCTS, CISSP, E|CEH, E|CSA, Security+, Cloud Essentials Certified, Mobility+, Network+, Cloud+, and CASP. You can follow Yuri on Twitter *@yuridiogenes* or read his articles on his personal blog at *http://aka.ms/yuridio*.

 JEFF GILBERT is a Senior Solutions Content Developer for the Cloud & Enterprise Division at Microsoft. From his office outside Boston, he authors cross-product solutions to IT business problems involving enterprise client management technologies, including Microsoft System Center Configuration Manager, Microsoft Intune, and Microsoft Desktop Optimization Pack (MDOP) products. In addition to local user groups, Jeff has been a speaker on enterprise client management and MDOP technologies at several conferences over the years, including the Microsoft Management Summit (MMS) and TechEd. Previous to this role, Jeff was the content publishing manager for MDOP and a senior technical writing lead for the Configuration Manager 2007 documentation team. Before joining Microsoft, Jeff was an SMS 2.0/SMS 2003 administrator with the US Army. You can follow Jeff on Twitter *@jeffgilb*.

From technical overviews to drilldowns on special topics, get *free* ebooks from Microsoft Press at:

www.microsoftvirtualacademy.com/ebooks

Download your free ebooks in PDF, EPUB, and/or Mobi for Kindle formats.

Look for other great resources at Microsoft Virtual Academy, where you can learn new skills and help advance your career with free Microsoft training delivered by experts.

Microsoft Press

Now that you've read the book...

Tell us what you think!

Was it useful?
Did it teach you what you wanted to learn?
Was there room for improvement?

Let us know at http://aka.ms/tellpress

Your feedback goes directly to the staff at Microsoft Press,
and we read every one of your responses. Thanks in advance!